GIMME

RH CHEVAL

DEDICATION

To those who have offered assistance, support, and encouragement, especially my partner and family, thank you.

CONTENTS

ACKNOWLEDGMENTS

For hard facts and well-reasoned opinion, there are a handful of print and TV journalists and commentators who provide an antidote to the mindless myths propagated by the so-called mainstream media. I'd like to especially acknowledge the work of *New York Post* columnist Michael Goodwin and contributors Betsey McCaughey and Richard Lowry, who is editor-in-chief of *National Review*, that top-notch news magazine for which correspondent Kevin Williamson writes, and Fox News anchors Chris Wallace and Bret Baier and legal analysts Alan Dershowitz and Andrew Napolitano.

1 GIMME GREEN

"We can just print more money"—Alexandria Ocasio-Cortez on funding the "Green New Deal"

Greenbacks

If you live in New York City or LA or San Francisco or Boston, you surely have neighbors or acquaintances that feel it's "unfair" that doctors and lawyers are "rich," but Starbucks "baristas" are not. They might agree with its former CEO, now considering running for president in 2020. The bigtime Democratic Party donor feels he doesn't pay his "fair share" of taxes. Of course, he could give the IRS more money without talking about it. He could point out that despite the 1% paying nearly all of our federal taxes, he agrees with Rep. Alexandria Ocasio-Cortez (AOC) that they're not paying their "fair share."

Liberals welcome the federal safety net, but some, like **Howard Schultz**, turn green when runaway Democratic Socialist AOC talks about raising the top tax rate to 70% for incomes over $10 million, or when socialist Senator Bernie Sanders proposes a tax of 77% on the estates of the wealthy, or when progressive presidential candidates line up to offer freebies to everyone. Billionaire Schultz was expected to be another Michael Bloomberg and buy a nomination. But people forget that when Bloomberg first ran for New York City mayor to succeed Rudy Giuliani, the former Democrat did not win a primary to get on the Democratic ticket: he ran as a Republican. When Schultz said in January he'd run as an Independent, progressives screamed he'd split the liberal vote and throw the election to Trump.

The game has changed in the Democratic Party. Equal opportunity is passé. "Fair share" means a redistribution of income to the have-nots. "Fair share" means funding excessive government spending. "Fair share" means enriching the political elite, not the corporate elite. "Fair share" means ending acquired, not earned wealth. Progressives demand that inheritance taxes be confiscatory not merely punitive, with the bulk of inherited wealth transferred to the government. Watch PBS's "Downton Abbey" with Maggie Smith. By the end of the series, in the pre-World War II era, severe taxation levied on aristocratic estates in the UK necessitates the breakup of most large land-holdings. Slices of estates are rented or sold, or converted to museums. That's what social justice means—it's justice with an ax saw. Or, in the real world of socialism and communism—the former Soviet republics, today's Venezuela and Cuba—what's yours is mine, and what's mine is mine, as they used to say on Israeli kibbutzim.

The Democratic Party no longer touts its zillionaire supporters. During the Bill Clinton era in the 1990s, "*the party became more dependent on glitzy Hollywood fundraisers, financiers, trial lawyers, and, eventually Silicon Valley,*" observed *National Review*'s Jim Geraghty (3/11/19), noting that from 1990 to 2010, the party and its candidates never received less than 42% of donations from Wall Street.

Elizabeth Warren's "wealth tax" would hit assets including physical property worth more than $50 million. They would be taxed at 2%. Assets above 1 billion—that's folks like Jeff Bezos, Michael Bloomberg, Bill Gates, Warren Buffet—would be taxed at 3%. Senator Warren would use the tax to pay for universal child-care.

If you're ambitious and greedy as well as socialist, get in with the political movers and shakers. Every true-blue socialist should own a vacation home— perhaps, a dacha on the lake-- as does schlump **Bernie Sanders**, who can afford to donate the bar mitzvah suit he still wears to Goodwill. During the 2016 campaign, "*his Royal Majesty King Bernie Sanders would only deign to leave his plush DC office or his brand-new second home on the lake if he was flown around on a cushy private jet like a billionaire master of the universe,*" groused Zac Petkanas of the Clinton campaign to *Politico*. The frequent fancy flier of fuel-guzzling private jets now promises to take on the fossil-fuel industry. The former Stalinist (see RH Cheval's *The SLJ: Self-Loathing Jews in America*) wants to expand the death tax by increasing rates from 40% to 77% and levying it on smaller estates worth $3.5 million—many New York condos are worth that—rather than its current target of property worth $11 million. Bye-bye, birdie.

If you're thinking this would pay for new socialist entitlements, you'd be wrong. Sanders' own estimates, reports *NR*, projects $32 billion in new revenue, *"less than 1 percent of the cost of the monopoly health-care scheme he is proposing"* (2/25/19). So, what's the purpose? It's another kind of green: envy. Taking away goodies from those who have more than you, gives numerous people, not just the literal have-nots, great pleasure, a variant of schadenfreude.

TV actor **Jussie Smollett** lost the last of his fan club when Chicago police not only disclosed that he orchestrated and paid for the so-called "hate attack" on himself and wrote the previous hate letter to himself, but did so because he was dissatisfied with his income on "Empire," reported to be $100,000/episode. Had he not been dumped from the last two episodes, he would have earned $1.8 million this season. That figure would put Smollett among the highest-earning 0.1% of all Americans, according to WhatsMyPercent.com, an online income percentile calculator that uses US Census Bureau data (*NYP*, 2/22/19). If progressives dislike corporate greed, they don't tolerate personal greed much better—unless it's a failing of political icons such as the Clintons.

In mid-February, Sanders said he was running for president to transform the Democratic Party and the nation. The party has already adopted his socialist program. Some are playing it cute. Senator **Kamala Harris** (D-CA) said she's not a Democratic Socialist although she jumped on the Green New Deal bandwagon. When asked on "The Breakfast Club" radio show in February whether as a former prosecutor she opposed legalizing pot, she replied: *"That's not true. And look, I joke about it—half joking—half my family is from Jamaica. Are you kidding me?"* Her father, Stanford economics professor Donald Harris, berated her in a statement to Jamaica Global Online (published on February 15th) for his family's *"name, reputation, and proud Jamaican identity being connected, in any way, jokingly or not, with the fraudulent stereotype of a pot-smoking joy seeker and in the pursuit of identity politics."*

Bernie says he is a democratic socialist, which isn't forthright either. He seems to mean the US should emulate Scandinavia. Other so-called socialists refer to redistribution of wealth and worker or government control of industry. As we see in Venezuela, socialism doesn't really mean democracy or justice or the same benefits for all. It means power for the ruling class, which is the political class. Just ask the starving people, the doctors and teachers turning to prostitution in order to eat as Nicolas Madura, whom Bernie Sanders wouldn't call a dictator when talking to CNN's Wolf Blitzer, refuses to abdicate and blocks humanitarian aid from crossing the border with Colombia or Brazil. The military are mostly standing by Madura, using force to ensure that neither food nor medicine reach the country of 30 million, some 3 million of whom have already fled, including, reports Fox News, 55% of Venezuela's physicians. Vice President Mike Pence announced new sanctions against 4 Venezuelan governors connected to Madura and asked the Lima Group of Latin American nations and Canada to freeze assets of that state-owned oil company, PDVSA, after clashes with the military killed 4, wounded more than 300, and blocked delivery by US-backed convoys of humanitarian aid. Nationwide power outages began on March 7th, patients in hospitals began dying, starving Venezuelans began looting grocery stores in Caracas on March 11th. On March 21st, opposition leader Juan Guaido's aide, lawyer Roberto Marrero, was kidnapped following a raid at his Caracas home. In late March, 80% of Venezuelans were without electricity.

Income Inequality

Although Oxfam International claimed a global "*inequality crisis*," income distribution is less unequal than it's been for a century, Bjorn Lomborg, director of the Copenhagen Consensus Center, observed last year: Asia's growth has led to the decline in global inequality for several decades. Income inequality has risen recently, as the top 1% of income in English-speaking countries "*has returned to levels akin to those in the early 1900s, while in non-English countries it has declined dramatically*" (NYP, 1/26/18). While it's true that inequality in wealth in individual countries has increased, it "*overstates the case when it claims that the wealth of the 42 richest people is greater than the bottom 50 percent of the planet (3.7 billion).*" How so? Nearly 1/5th of the bottom half have debts adding up to $1.2 trillion—such as students with loans who hardly can be said to be poor.

Income inequality in the US has been growing since the 1970s. The one-percenters received 20% of pretax income in 2013, as compared to 10% from 1950 – 1980. The crème-de-la crème—the top 0.1% of households—received about 10% of the pretax income in 2013, but only 3%-4% between 1951 and 1981. In the recovery period following the 2008 recession, income inequality grew further. The Congressional Budget Office (CBO) reported in November, 2014 that the share of pretax income received by the top 1% rose from 13.3% in 2009 to 14.6% in 2011. Another estimate is that the one-percenters' share of income rose from 12% in 1980 to 20% in 2014. The bottom half of the US population accounted for 20% of incomes in 1980 but declined to 12% in 2014. The new 2018 Republican tax law addresses stagnant middle-class incomes by increasing the standard deduction (to $12,000 for an individual, $24,000 for a married couple), reducing tax rates (the top rate was lowered to 37%; the bottom remained at 10%, with income thresholds adjusted and most taxpayers seeing lower rates), and promoting growth through lower corporate tax rates.

Liberal Fox News analyst, Juan Williams, notes that 1% of Americans control 40% of wealth in the US. The top 1% paid nearly half (45.7%) of federal income tax for 2014, the largest share in at least 3 years, reported Robert Frank (14/14/15, www.cnbc.com). Currently, the bottom 50% pay 3% of total taxes (Fox News, 3/28/19). The top 0.1% of families pay the equivalent of 39.2% of federal income tax, according to the Pew Research Center (PRC), while the bottom 20% have "*negative tax rates*," meaning they get more money back from the government in refundable tax credits than they pay in taxes. (Be careful not to criticize those who pay no taxes. You never know when you may run for office and your words, like 2012 presidential candidate Mitt Romney's, may come back to bite you.) The CBO found that the share of federal taxes paid by the top 1% of earners has dramatically increased since 1979 as the one-percenters' share of earnings has also increased. In 1979, one-percenters earned 8.9% of pretax income and paid 18% of federal income taxes. In 2011, one-percenters earned 14.6% of income and paid 25.4% of federal income taxes. The federal income tax rate paid by the top 1% dropped from 22.7% in 1979 to 20.3% in 2011.

Hot off the press: in 2018 there were 11.8 million US households with a net worth of more than $1 million, comprising 3% of the population, although the rate of achieving millionaire status is slowing. For the 10th straight year the number of US millionaires has gone up (according to Market Insights Report by the research firm Spectrem, which excluded primary residence from net worth), with a quarter of a million households joining the millionaires' club in 2018. Some 1.3 million Americans achieved multimillionaire status—household assets worth $5 million - $25 million. Only 173,000 households met their idea of crème-de-la-crème: a net worth above $25 million.

In the US a larger percentage of government revenue comes from income tax than in other countries that rely more on consumption taxes. Individual income taxes account for 47.4% of government revenue, a share that has been constant since World War II (Drew DeSilver, PRC, 4/13/16). The federal government collected $91.54 trillion from individual income taxes in fiscal year 2015, its single largest source of revenue. The progressive US income tax system relies on the wealthy, who rely on the stock market.

In fiscal year 2015, the feds collected 10.6% of its total revenue from corporate income taxes (some $348.3 billion). At 21%, under the new Trump tax law, the corporate tax rate is now competitive. Following passage of the Trump tax cut, there was a surge in the GDP, company bonuses, and pay hikes. Wages have been rising in more than 40% of cities. *"This is not a story of the rich getting richer,"* wrote Michael Hendrix in *NR*. *"The least well-paid and least educated Americans in the work force are seeing proportionally bigger wage gains nationwide."* Unemployment is at a 45-year low (about 4%), and also at an historic low for African-Americans, and regulations are being rolled back.

The wealthiest Americans pay the lion's share of federal income taxes. Those making under $15,000 in adjusted gross income (AGI) in 2014 made up more than 24% of total tax returns but only 0.1% of the income taxes paid (PRC). In 2014, those with an AGI of $250,000 or more paid 51.6% of all individual income taxes but accounted for only 2.7% of all returns filed. Those who earned under $50,000 accounted for 62.3% of individual returns filed but paid just 5.7% of total taxes. Those making between $100,000 - $200,000 paid 23.8% of the total tax liability in 2011, but only 18.8% in 2000; those earning between $50,000 - $75,000 paid 12% of total tax liability in 2000 but only 9.1% in 2011.

Since 1970, the federal revenue source that's grown the most is the payroll tax. Since the 6.2% Social Security withholding tax applies only to wages up to $118,500, everyone but the top earning 20% of American families pay more in payroll taxes than in federal income taxes, according to a Treasury Department analysis.

What's your "fair share?" Few will think they're not paying enough. Drew DeSilver ends his 2016 article for Pew with a quote attributed to the finance minister of Louis XIV, Jean Baptiste Colbert: *"The art of taxation consists in so plucking the goose as to obtain the largest possible amount of feathers with the smallest possible amount of hissing."* But the goose can also be force-fed to make *foie gras*. That's cruelty to the goose and outlawed in Europe, and that's cruelty to the taxpayer forced to pay a boat load of taxes, and that's what's happening in over-taxed blue states.

New York State revenue also relies on the wealthy, which is why the governor regrets that higher state taxes are chasing away its high-earners, leading to a shortfall in revenue. Governor **Andrew Cuomo** saw revenue drop as the Trump tax reform put a cap on $10,000 in state and local taxes that could be deducted from federal taxes. The city with the highest state and local taxes in the nation is aghast that its people are fleeing to Florida, which (along with 6 other states) has no income tax. The top 1% of earners on average deducted $500,000/year for state and local taxes. Only 34% of New York filers and 40% of Connecticut and New Jersey filers itemized before the new Republican tax law, notes former New York State Lt. Governor, Betsey McCaughey.

Did the high-tax state reduce its taxes? Of course not. New York continues to spend like a drunken sailor as millionaires head for Texas, Arizona, and Florida. In early February 2019 the governor and Comptroller Tom DiNapoli announced that projected income-tax revenue for the year dropped $2.3 billion. *"Tax the rich! Tax the rich! Tax the rich! We did. Now, God forbid, the rich leave,"* said Cuomo. The top 1% of the state's earners provide 46% of the state's personal-income-tax revenues. Census data show that New Yorkers began heading to low tax states long before Trump's tax bill.

Mayor **Bill de Blasio**'s boondoggles cost billions. In February 2019, the mayor admitted he blew nearly $773 million on a "**Renewal**" school program over 5 years on which he was now pulling the plug. In late February, the City Council was shocked to learn that New York's First Lady **Chirlane McCray**'s ill-defined mental health endeavor, "**ThriveNYC**," had spent

$850 million in 4 years. The situation with the mentally ill is *"actually getting worse,"* said Robert Holden (D-Queens) at a City Council meeting on February 27th. Council Speaker Corey Johnson on WNYC's "The Brian Lehrer Show," spoke about *"how to help the severely mentally ill people…you see on the streets and on the subways."* A *Politico* report indicated that Thrive doesn't track results or spending, and doesn't provide greater access for inpatient treatment or intensive outpatient services for the seriously mentally ill. Officials can't even cite details of what they paid for, yet the program is to receive $250 million/year more to spend over the next 4 years. John Snook, director of the nonprofit Treatment Advocacy Center, writes that only 4.6% in the state's county mental health system received wraparound services, while more than $133.5 million was spent on *"stress reduction."*

On Fox 5's "Good Day New York" on March 6th Roseanna Scotto observed, *"We are still seeing a lot of homeless on the street. And apparently not a lot of bookkeeping from your office."* Guest McCray babbled, *"That is absolutely not true. We have so many measures in place. And, um, you know, so many things."* Homelessness also plagues San Francisco, which frames the issue as the need for more low-cost housing rather treatment of serious mental illness and substance abuse. In New York City, the number of mentally ill homeless has spiked from 9,840 in 2015, when Thrive began, to over 12,140 (US Dept. of HUD). Thrive targets neither the seriously mentally ill on the streets nor in jail.

When co-host Lori Stokes wanted to know what's been accomplished for all the money, McCray talked about spending only $560 million by the end of June. The only Thrive initiative she mentioned was its helpline. Later, at the Brooklyn Museum, she gave some statistics on helpline calls, screening for postpartum depression, and crime victims referred for counselling. At a Midwood senior center, she announced a $1.7 million plan to expand mental-health services for such centers. *"There's no evidence it's working,"* said City Councilman Ritchie Torres (D-Bx). McCray's response to critics: *"Haters gonna hate."*

Mayor de Blasio tried damage control on the same show (3/13/19), touting his failures as successes. State assemblywoman Nicole Malliotakis (R-B'klyn/SI) recites some of his failures in the *Post* (3/15/19): the city has the highest tax burden in the nation, property taxes have soared 44% since he became mayor, the homeless population has grown to 76,000, the subways and schools are a disaster, too many storefronts are empty due to high rents, sex crimes are up (so are murders), public spaces are marred by addicts shooting up, litter, and urination, and NYCHA, with a *"tenant population slightly larger than the city of Cleveland"* is treated with *"malign bureaucratic neglect."*

Mayor de Blasio flipped when hedge fund mogul Ken Griffin spent $238 million for a 25,000 Central Park Avenue South apartment. The City Council proposed a pied-à-terre tax to deal with such purchases which Mark Levine, a sponsor of the bill, called *"grotesque."* But it's deals like Griffin's *"that keep the city from going broke,"* notes *New York Post*'s Steve Cuozzo (2/5/19). *"It might not seem 'fair' for one individual to spend so much money for a four-story castle in the sky when millions of New Yorkers struggle to afford basic housing,"* Cuozzo observes, *"what's truly 'grotesque' is the scandalous condition of NYCHA, home to more than 400,000 of the city's poorest residents,"* who've spent the winter without heat. But wouldn't you know it Dems love the idea of a pied-à-terre tax to filch non-residents and fund the MTA.

Another tax the city is getting ready to levy in 2020 is **congestion pricing** in Manhattan below 61st Street to salvage the crumbling, unsafe, and unreliable subway system. Both the governor and mayor are on board and state legislators agreed although they see the fee starting at $12/day for a car, $25 for a truck, about $3,500 a year, as punitive to outer-borough and suburban drivers. Revenues would go right down the MTA toilet because management won't touch bloated union contracts. As an alternative means of financing mass transit—perish the thought that riders themselves pay for the costs of running the subway-- New York Assembly Speaker Carl Heastie suggests raising another regressive consumption tax, the state sales tax on gasoline. In 2018, the combined federal and state gas tax per gallon amounted to nearly 64 cents, the 5th highest in the nation, with the state collecting $1.6 billion in gas-related taxes last year.

In early March, New Jersey's Governor **Phil Murphy** proposed a "millionaire's tax," that would lower the income threshold for the top tax rate of 10.75% from $5 million to $1 million to target some 39,000 taxpayers, up from under 2,000 taxpayers. He'd up spending, too. 60% of Jersey's income tax revenue comes from the wealthy, and tax revenues are lower than anticipated because income-tax revenue is down more than 5%. Bear in mind that New Jersey has the highest property taxes in the nation. Democratic state Senate President Steve Sweeney observed that in *"overtaxed"* Jersey, *"The people who can leave are leaving."*

Here a tax, there a tax, everywhere a tax. That's the only way Democrats know how to govern. Progressives add to the misery of consumers and businesses by throwing in demands for unionization, more regulations, and payoffs to local pols. Taxes are driving out the middle-class. A Quinnipiac poll on March 20, 2019 found that 41% of New York City residents said they'll be forced to leave the state in the next 5 years. According to a survey by real-estate Web site StreetEasy, the median cost of a home is $637,000, nearly 3 times the national average of $230,000.

Single-payer Medicare-for-All advocate **Kirsten Gillibrand** has proposed—you guessed it—another tax, a 4% tax on income, which critics estimate would fall short by about $2 trillion a year. Her pandering is coming to naught since she got caught in the #Me Too web. A female staffer resigned after Gillibrand sided with a male aide, Abbas Malik, accused of sexual harassment, a complaint investigated by her office. He was fired in early March before the *Politico* story was published.

Equal pay for equal work is a pithy slogan. In January 2018 Hollywood was "outraged" that after actor Christopher Plummer was hired to replace accused sexual predator Kevin Spacey, Mark Wahlberg was paid $1.5 million to reshoot scenes in "All the Money in the World" but co-star Michelle Williams got less than $1,000 for the 10 days of shooting. She needs a better agent.

Sometimes the work isn't really equal. A different title, different job responsibilities, longer hours and more traveling by singles than married moms. This is a contentious issue that rarely brings a smile. In an equal pay lawsuit, a Ninth Circuit Court of Appeals in California ruling by Judge Steven Reinhardt that employers may not use past salaries to justify pay differentials under the federal Equal Pay Act was invalidated by the High Court because it was issued 11 days after his death on March 29, 2018. Never say that the Supremes are humorless. On February 25th, the unsigned High Court opinion noted that *"Federal judges are appointed for life, not for eternity."* The judge's passing before the decision was filed meant the lower court *"erred in counting him as a member of the majority."* With approval by only 5 of 10 members of the lower court, the case went back to the 9th Circuit.

Bridging income inequality invites far-fetched schemes by presidential aspirants beholden to identity politics. In February, Senator **Kamala Harris** (D-CA) endorsed reparations for descendants of black slavery to address "*inequities*": "*people aren't starting out on the same base in terms of their ability to succeed, and so we have got to recognize that and give people a lift up*," she said on "The Breakfast Club" radio show. She told the *New York Times*, she would "*make real investments in black communities*." Senator Elizabeth Warren was equally vague in talking about reparations for slavery and discrimination "*that has had many consequences, including undermining the ability of black families to build wealth in America*."

Green Energy

AOC's "Green New Deal" made its debut as a parody of a progressive wish list. House Speaker Nancy Pelosi scoffed it off for its "enthusiasm." 2020 Democratic contenders Senators Kamala Harris (CA), Cory Booker (NJ), and Kirsten Gillibrand (NY) embraced it. It contains a litany of freebies: education, health-care, and a living wage for all including freeloaders unwilling to work. That last bit, a bonanza for Republicans, was quickly removed from AOC's website. Someone said that Senate Majority Leader Mitch McConnell (R-KY) likes the Green New Deal even more than AOC.

The "green" in AOC's New Deal stands not for greenbacks but clean energy, "*100 percent of the power demand in the United States through clean, renewable, and zero-emissions energy sources*," within 10 years. The GND calls for public ownership of green projects, "*guaranteeing a job*," and "*high-quality health care*." What government-administered health care is high-quality? Not England's. Not Israel's 50 years ago when socialism was dominant. With all the bennies socialists wish to extend, there's no thought of where the money will come from once the oil and gas industry is destroyed, air travel made obsolete, all homes in America retrofitted with clean energy devices. Private health insurance covered by employers would be abolished in Kamala Harris's proposal as well as in Sanders' Medicare-for-All scheme. That would affect some 217 million Americans who have a private health plan as well as another 18 million enrolled in Medicare Advantage plans.

What's in a name? *NR* says the GND was outmoded when Obama was pushing it, and when Tom Friedman before him (credited with coining the phrase in 2007), and *"when the Communist Party USA was pushing it before him"* (3/11/19). No sooner had AOC presented her ideals than the very progressive newly elected Governor of California **Gavin Newsom** dashed them to smithereens with the best line ever: *"Let's be real."* He threw in the towel on his high-speed railway from LA to San Francisco, for which Obama provided federal funds in his stimulus package, the bullet-speed trains that are AOC's clean-energy alternative to air travel. Or as conservative radio megastar Rush Limbaugh would say on Fox News Sunday (2/17/19), the plan replaces planes with *"a train to Hawaii."* Newsom said the project would *"cost too much and take too long"*—now projected at $77 billion (the *New York Post* claims the real cost is $117 billion) and the Department of Defense (DOD) postponed to 2033-- and had been mismanaged, but since he still fancies the idea, he won't return the $3.5 billion in federal money already spent to the Trump administration. *"If high-speed rail is not feasible in the state with the three densest major metro areas in the nation, and the highest overall urban density, it is not feasible anywhere in the United States,"* declared Joel Kotkin and Wendell Cox in *City Journal*.

President Trump has said often enough that the world's major polluters would go on polluting if the US curtailed its carbon emissions in compliance with an international agreement such as the Paris Accord. Megan McArdle, columnist for *The Washington Post* (2/18/19), agrees that the problem with advocates of the Green New Deal is that *"like all myopes,"* they *"can see clearly only what's right in front of them, which is to say the United States, beyond which they perceive only the fuzzy outlines of a half-mythical European enviro-paradise."* She objects to the outdated, US-centric approach taken in the resolution by Rep. AOC and Sen. Edward Markey (D-MA) because today the US accounts for 4.3% of world population, 25% of its economic output, and only 15% of global carbon emissions from combustion, while China, with 18% of the world's population, has 15% of its gross domestic product and 28% of its emissions. Populous India produces only 3% of global GDP and 6% of emissions. Billions of people in these developing countries, McArdle argues, will pass through a stage when their industries are much dirtier than their highly-regulated rich-world counterparts: *"The global emissions is likely to get much worse before it gets any better."* An energy-efficient US *"won't prevent the planet warming"* because the *"problem is the more than 6 billion people who aren't living in the rich world"* and developing countries *"aren't going to put scarce resources into artificially expensive 'green' ways of replicating the rich-world lifestyle; they're going to get there by the least costly route."*

The solution, McArdle offers, is to figure out how to make "green" measures cheaper than carbon-intensive versions. The solution is not *"massive regulatory programs to marginally improve the energy efficiency of American buildings,"* nor *"subsidizing high-speed rail and public transit in a country almost entirely devoid of the population densities needed to make them feasible;"* nor *"larding green initiatives with ideological wish lists that will do nothing to prevent climate change"* but will polarize the country—the route chosen by the Green New Dealers. Amen to that.

Targets of doomsday propaganda are not only conservative skeptics but level-headed liberals such as veteran Senator **Dianne Feinstein**. On February 22nd, a group called the Sunrise Movement used kids to confront Feinstein and demand support for the GND. She stood her ground, saying it's unaffordable and telling the kids that *"I've been doing this for 30 years"* and *"I know what I'm doing."* She chided the GND supporters, *"You come in here and you say, 'It has to be my way or the highway.' I don't respond to that."* AOC proved her right, talking about climate change being *"a dire threat to humanity"* and mocking Feinstein. On February 25th, the Sunrise Movement marched on the office of Senator Majority Leader Mitch McConnell, who would be only too happy to have a vote on the Green New Deal. And what a vote it was on March 26th, with not a single Democrat voting for the GND measure. Even co-sponsor Senator Ed Markey (D-MA) joined 42 other Dems in voting "present" while 6 Dems and all Republicans voted "nay."

In keeping with the spirit of liberal hypocrisy, AOC, *"addicted to Uber,"* as the *Post* put it, *"made her get-away from a St. Patrick's Day parade in Queens in a fuel-hogging, for-hire van"* on Sunday, March 3rd, although she was less than 4 blocks from a subway station. Her campaign shelled out nearly $30,000 in Uber and other taxi rides but only $12,000 on subway rides and trains. She's quick to take a plane rather than a train. Mean green sacrifices are for the hoi polloi just as paying taxes were for "the little people," not Leona Helmsley. The *Washington Examiner* on March 5th reported that a conservative government watchdog, the National Legal and Policy Center, filed a complaint with the Federal Election Commission alleging her campaign manager, now chief of staff millionaire Saikat Chakrabarti, moved more than

$1 million in political donations into 2 of his own companies, Brand New Congress LLC, and Brand New Campaign LLC, to evade reporting requirements by PACs, and perhaps violated campaign-finance laws in exceeding the $5,000 limit on donations from PACs to candidates. The lawyer for the warrior against "dark money" counters that the FEC doesn't require disclosure of the information.

The Green New Deal & Amazon

The Green New Deal promises in a decade to wipe out our economy in its lust to end corporate greed. What is meant by corporate greed? Companies such as Amazon. The deal to put up HQ2 in Long Island City, cooked in the back room by New York Governor Andrew Cuomo and Mayor Bill de Blasio, irked the would-be local king-makers. They killed the deal with contempt, push for unionization, and the prospect of riling Jeff Bezos with never-ending impositions. AOC rejoiced that corporate greed got its comeuppance from little her and her allies. New York's political socialists hated the deal; the majority of New Yorkers wanted the 25,000 high-paying jobs Amazon promised the city in exchange for $3 billion in state and local tax breaks. (A February Sienna poll found 58% of registered city voters and 70% of black voters favored the plan, opposed by 35%). The project was estimated to bring in $27 billion in tax revenue to New York over 25 years and would also generate 1,300 construction jobs per year during the 15-year building timeframe.

Cuomo's requirement that Amazon use union labor to construct its headquarters, for which it would receive a $500 million taxpayer grant, had to be ratified by a state panel that deputy state senate majority leader **Mike Gianaris** (D-LIC) was appointed to—a signal to Amazon of dark days ahead. Gianaris was described by an unnamed Queens politician as a "scaredy cat" because of the AOC surprise victory in June 2018 over Joe Crowley. Amazon said polls showed 70% of New Yorkers supported their plans, while "*a number of state and local politicians have made it clear that they oppose our presence and will not work with us to build the type of relationships that are required to go forward with the project we and many others envisioned in Long Island City.*"

On Twitter, Rep. Alexandria Ocasio-Cortez gloated: "*Anything is possible: Today was the day a group of dedicated, everyday New Yorkers & their neighbors defeated Amazon's corporate greed, its worker exploitation, and the power of the richest man in the world."*

"No, everyday New Yorkers did not do it," objected Peggy Noonan in the *Wall Street Journal* (2/23-2/24/19). *"They wanted the jobs. It was you, Fredo."* On WNYC radio, uber-progressive de Blasio took AOC to task for inspiring the Amazon pullout: *"I'll take on any progressive anywhere that thinks it's a good idea to lose jobs and revenue because I think that's out of touch with what working people want."* The mayor recalled the bad old days— *"what happened in this city when it almost went to bankruptcy in the 1970s."* In a Twitter response on February 15th, AOC preached progressive purity: *"Come for me all you want, but my job is to make sure that people are protected in society. Someone's got to look out for the people our system is leaving behind – esp now, when most of the wealth created is going to fewer people, those left behind are the majority of Americans."* AOC refused to accept blame for defeating the deal, but a Sienna College poll on March 18th showed that 38% of state voters cast her as the "villain" (34% blamed local activists, 29% the mayor, 28% the governor, and 26% Amazon).

The Amazon debacle was not just a loss, wrote Noonan, but *"a whole lost world"* and *"watershed event"* after which *"no major American company will open a new headquarters here for at least a generation … because the politicians you're making the deal with can't control their own troops"* in a town *"whose political life is dominated by a wild and rising progressive left."* Her advice: *"You don't unleash the furies and hold hearings where crowds jeer, hiss and chant, 'GTFO, Amazon has got to go.' … You don't become Tweeting Trotsky."* Progressives *"let their prey go,"* Noonan cries. *"What second-rate slobs run this town."*

The humiliating defeat for Governor Cuomo means the end of his presidential aspirations. Cuomo reports more than $2 billion in tax shortfalls because the rich are heading south and west. Cuomo called Gianaris' opposition *"political malpractice"* and on Valentine's Day also blamed other state officials: *"The New York state Senate has done tremendous damage. They should be held accountable for this lost economic opportunity."* That's what happens when Democrats have a monopoly in government.

If given a second chance, Cuomo promised to shepherd the Amazon deal through the state legislature, where senate majority leader Andrea Stewart-Cousins (D-Yonkers) said she'd work with Amazon—Gianiris was off the panel-- but pointed to *"serious flaws in our economic-development programs that need to be reformed."* Then came the "Dear Jeff" letter, a full-page ad in the

Times on March 1st signed by labor and community leaders, business groups, and legislators asking Bezos to reconsider. It began: *"New Yorkers do not want to give up on the 25,000 permanent jobs, 11,000 union construction and maintenance jobs, and $28 billion in new tax revenues that Amazon was prepared to bring to our state. A clear majority of New Yorkers support his project and were disappointed by your decision not to proceed. We understand that becoming home to the world's industry leader in e-commerce, logistics and web services would be a tremendous boost for our state's technology industry, which is our fastest growing generator of new jobs."* In other words, we're sorry you ditched us. No deal on appeal.

Political malpractice is a term many New Yorkers throw at the governor, whose upstate boondoggles have failed at great cost, with too many of his colleagues being outfitted for jail jumpsuits. Two days before the Amazon pullout, Cuomo's economic-development czar, Howard Zemsky, admitted that Cuomo's $750 million taxpayer gamble on a Buffalo, New York solar-panel plant run by Panasonic and Tesla had bombed. Cuomo landed just 700 jobs at the plant, noted a *Post* editorial (2/16/19), while *"the feds convicted multiple close Cuomo associates of corruption tied to the Buffalo Billion projects."*

Real-estate columnist at the *Post*, Steve Cuozzo, said of Amazon's foes, *"Having gotten their way, they'll surely set their sights on more targets. JPMorgan, which still needs City Council approval for 270 Park Ave. [for a new headquarters tower], had better be on guard."* Development projects require air-rights transfers, rezoning for affordable housing construction, waterfront public parks—all of which *"are 'exploitive' in the eyes of the Ocasio-Cortez crowd."*

On Friday, March 15, 2019, the nation's largest private real-estate project opened on the West Side, **Hudson Yards**, built by Related Companies and Oxford Properties Group, made possible by former Mayor **Michael Bloomberg**. The *Times* in its March 10th Sunday complained of the $6 billion subsidies for the 28-acre project of high-rise office buildings, residential towers, performance arts center, public school, mall, restaurants, retail stores, spiral "Vessel," and the highest outdoor observation deck in this hemisphere. The $6 billion, Cuozzo reported was actually distributed across the 360-acre district where more than a dozen developers are involved, and more than a third of that, a *Post* editorial (3/13/19) noted, was for extension of the #7 subway, while nearly all the rest was for *"reductions in future tax collections"*. Fox 5 reported the project has already created 50,000 jobs.

Progressives who hate progress should think of the tourist influx and tax revenue if not New York's skyline.

The War Against Tech

City officials *"don't want new technology-based industries like Airbnb to succeed without their strict oversight,"* writes Jonathan S. Tobin (NYP, 2/27/19), noting that *"With Airbnb and other home-sharing apps, hotels and their unions fear the competition. With Uber and Lyft, it's the taxi industry and medallion owners."* New York laws against high-tech businesses *"exist primarily to protect entrenched interests."* City Journal's Joel Kotkin and Wendell Cox report that a new study shows that New York now suffers *"the largest net annual outmigration of post-college millennials"* of any metro region.

It's not just New York City officials. Far-left **Elizabeth Warren** wants to break up high tech giants, Amazon, Google, and Facebook, all major political donors, to give a boost to competition and better protect our privacy. *"We have these giant tech companies that think they rule the Earth,"* Warren said in Queens on March 8th. *"They've bulldozed competition, used our private information for profit, and tilted the playing field for everybody else."* Warren has accepted at least $90,000 from workers at the tech companies between 2011 and 2018 ($2,700 from Facebook COO Sherly Sandberg, *Politico* reported). Amazon has infuriated progressives who complain of its low wages, as well as Barnes & Nobles, now on life support, and retailers. Google defeats smaller companies in battles over search-engine ad placements, and has been fined nearly $2 billion by European Commissioner for Competition Margrethe Vestager for past coercion of sites that use Google to display only its ads. Warren later added Apple to her hit list. Social media has been criticized for permitting election interference and Facebook has mishandled users' data as if it were their own.

A story on Hoda Muthana, suing to come back to the US from Syria, was headlined: *"How jihadi tweets inspired US 'ISIS bride'."* She began using Twitter after graduating high school in 2013 and became radicalized by other Islamic State supporters. Twitter and Facebook and YouTube have been criticized for failing to stop extremists from using their platforms to recruit new terrorists and post anti-American propaganda. In 2015, Twitter reported that it had suspended 10,000 ISIS-linked accounts, and by February, 2016 some 125,000 accounts had been shuttered.

Facebook has come into criticism since the 2016 election when Russian trolls posing as Americans posted incendiary comments on social media. A US Air Force intelligence officer Monica Elfriede Witt revealed what feds call *"a highly classified intelligence program"* to Iran and helped it to try to hack the computers of then-fellow agents. The Texas-native counterintelligence officer had been deployed on missions to the Middle East, spoke Farsi, shifted allegiance in Iran, and converted to Islam. She conducted multiple searches for agents using Facebook accounts using fake names, and Iranian hackers used the information to trick those agents into installing malware in their computers. Two Iranian firms are facing sanctions. De Witt, aka Fatemah Zahra and Narges Witt, remains at large on the FBI's most-wanted list.

The most recent horror story is the March 15th livestreaming on Facebook of a terrorist attack at 2 mosques in New Zealand (and spread to YouTube, Twitter, and Reddit) by a 28-year-old Australian white supremacist, Brenton Tarrant, who killed 50, injured 50, and posted a deranged anti-Muslim Manifesto. The video stayed up for an hour on Facebook and got nearly 200 views live, but about 4,000 before it was taken down. Some 24 hours later, Facebook removed all 1.5 million videos from its platform. YouTube said the video was being uploaded at the rate of nearly once per second in the 24 hours after the attack. YouTube temporarily disabled the ability to filter the uploaded video. Reddit banned 2 subreddits.

According to his 74-page manifesto, the terrorist chose New Zealand to show that *"nowhere in the world was safe."* He called Trump a symbol of *"renewed white identity and common purpose"* yet approved of Communist China. The massacre appeared to be inspired by ISIS, with the Christchurch attacker playing a Serbian song *"that salutes the 1995 butcher of Muslims, Radovan Karadzic,"* notes Tom Rogan of the *Washington Examiner*. As usual, Democrats weaponized his rant to link it to Trump's rhetoric regarding an "invasion" of illegal immigrants. On "Fox News Sunday" (3/17/19), Acting Chief of Staff Mick Mulvaney called it *"absurd"* to blame a murderer's despicable rampage on Trump, saying he is not a *"white supremacist."* Tech companies got their fair share of blame. Margaret Sullivan at the *Washington Post* said, *"The social-media companies need to get far more serious about editing and removing hate and terror."* In response, Facebook expressed its intent to block content suggestive of white supremacism, setting the teeth of free speech advocates on edge.

Facebook is blamed for alleged violations of privacy. It came under fire after Cambridge Analytica, a consulting firm Trump used during the campaign, gained access to the private data of more than 50 million users. In February 2019, the FCC received a complaint that Facebook failed to protect health data in its groups, and a House committee wanted CEO Mark Zuckerberg to address how sensitive medical information posted in supposedly private groups could be harvested.

In March 2018 Facebook was sued for using an algorithm that allegedly permits landlords and real-estate brokers to discriminate against women and other protected categories from receiving their housing ads. The National Fair Housing Alliance and 3 other advocacy groups filed suit in Manhattan federal court, alleging Mark Zuckerberg's advertising platform violates the Fair Housing Act and was caught red-handed in a sting operation: a sham company seeking housing ads in New York, DC, Miami and San Antonio used Facebook's platform to run ads that excluded users with children, the disabled, and speakers of English as a second language.

How many 2020 Democratic contenders will reject the nose-dive to the left? Senator **Amy Klobuchar** has stated, "*I am not for free college for all*" (CNN, 2/18/19). But she's co-sponsored the Green New Deal and calls for an expansion of Medicaid and Medicare. **Michael Bloomberg**, advocate of a nanny state, bowed out in early March, conceding he'd never win the Democratic primary (true), but bragging (falsely) that he'd beat Trump in a general election; he'll finance liberal candidates and causes. Perennial loser Hillary Clinton also dropped out, promising to never keep her opinions to herself. Former VP **Joe Biden**, a poll winner with name recognition but recently saddled with a sexual misconduct allegation, is so busy apologizing for his old-fashioned liberalism, he'll never make it to the finish line. Cynthia Nixon recently demanded he recant saying of VP Mike Pence—whom she calls "*America's most anti-LGBT elected official*" -- a "*decent guy*." Biden obliged. He's likely to pick a woman of color as VP (Stacey Abrams is interested in only the top spot), and sure to play at "Uncle Joe" despite, *Politico* tells us, a nearly $3 million vacation home, more than $100,000 a pop in speaking gigs, and lucrative book deal. We'll see if Joe endorses open borders and joins the radicals wanting to remake our political institutions: stacking the Supreme

Court, abolishing the Electoral College, and lowering the voting age to 16.

Funny how former bartender AOC's views on the access of money seem in cinq with that of Cybill Shepard's rich WASP sidekick, Maryann, played by Christine Baranski in the late-nineties' TV comedy "Cybill." Cybill would complain she ran out of money. Not to worry, Baranski would say (often with a martini in hand): There's an ATM down the block.

2 GIMME SOCIALISM

"America will never be a socialist country"—President Donald J. Trump, State of the Union Address

Our quasi-welfare state retains its capitalistic foundations. Sweden is often presented as a socialist country when it remains a liberal democratic welfare state. Most Western nations today are not bona fide socialist states with a coercive, centralized government in control of industry and banking, the central arbiter of wages and prices.

Gallup reports that 57% of Democrats have a positive view of socialism but the same respondents in the poll support small business and reject the notion that the government is doing too little, the *New York Post* writes in an editorial entitled "What is Socialism?" (3/4/19). Numerous millennials endorse socialism and Social Democrats such as AOC point to Scandinavia as "true socialism." At a rally in March, AOC basically defined capitalism as rapacious greed. She does not understand that in capitalism the means of production are controlled by the people; in socialism, the means of production—i.e., industry-- are controlled by the government—that's the system that's *"irredeemable,"* never wanting to relinquish power. While today's American socialists—AOC and Sanders—supposedly reject repressive states like the former Soviet Union, you don't hear AOC or Sanders criticize socialist regimes such as Venezuela's, about to collapse from Maduro's brutal and bankrupt dictatorship.

Nonetheless, whether it's safety-net benefits or ever-expanding administrative agencies such as the EPA or IRS or government control over much of our healthcare industry—Obamacare regulations regarding health insurance requirements, Medicaid, and Medicare—the US federal government today has a vastly larger footprint in our economy and political life than it did in the pre-Franklin Delano Roosevelt era.

European countries have more welfare-state features than the US. The US is the only OECD (Organization for Economic Cooperation and Development) country that doesn't have a federal paid-leave program. Sometimes a too-good-to-be-true benefit doesn't last. Germany in 2013 instituted a legal right to free child-care plus a stipend of about $200/month to stay-at-home moms, writes Patrick Brown (*NR*, 3/11/19). Two years later a German court declared the federal payment unconstitutional although 3 German states continue them at the state level.

C'est damage!

Democratic presidential candidates in 2020 are talking about guaranteed minimum incomes, raising the minimum wage even as companies fire workers to mitigate the cost, and job security. Job security in France contributes to social unrest as unemployment remains high, especially for Muslims. You can't fire the workers already entrenched. Riots continue in Paris and elsewhere across France, by so-called "yellow-vests" (that French law requires all drivers to wear in emergencies), initially over an increased fuel tax, but morphed into anti-government demonstrations.

What's the gripe? France has the highest ratio of tax revenue to gross national product (46.2%) of all OECD countries (the US—27.1%). It provides universal health care. It has a capitalist economy, thriving private sector, but high unemployment. Compared to the US worker, the French worker has been coddled, with a short work-week and extensive summer vacation.

But since November 17, 2018, through February 2019, there have been more than 8,000 arrests, more than 2,000 civilian injuries, more than a dozen fatalities, and more than 300,000 participants. Protestors blocked the roads; riots ensued. A violent protest in Paris on November 24th was blamed by the Minister of Interior on Marine Le Pen, Macron's right-wing opponent in 2017 presidential election, for urging protesters to go to the Champs Élysées. On December 1st, in the most violent riot in Paris since May 1968, more than 100 cars were burned, the Arc de Triomphe was vandalized, and the Louvre,

Eiffel Tower, and Paris Opera had to be closed. Police used grenades when necessary and tear-gas to subdue violent protesters.

The trigger was a proposed 2019 rise in fuel prices, especially diesel, to which a VAT tax is added, whose impact would fall on rural and exurban dwellers, who suffer high unemployment rates, not on the urban elite who can afford living in the big cities with mass transportation. Not needing a car has become a status symbol, opined a BBC report. Those in city centers enjoy public transit, *"but you need to be rich enough to live in the center of Paris or Marseilles or Bordeaux"* (*NYT*, 11/24/18). Demonstrators, some self-employed, complained of the high cost of living, low wages, and the onus of tax reforms shouldered by the working and middle classes. They demanded reinstatement of a tax on wealth that Macron scrapped on taking office, an increase in the minimum wage, the right to petition the government to enact or repeal a law, and Macron's departure. Extremists on both the right and left joined the *"gilets jaunes."* Galvanized through social media, the movement for economic justice has not been associated with a particular political party. In another explosion of violence along the Champs-Élysées, yellow-vest protests smashed luxury stores, set life-threatening fires that destroyed a bank, on Saturday, March 16th, in the 18th straight weekend of protests against Macron. *"How is the Paris Environmental Accord working out for France,"* President Trump tweeted on Saturday.

In December 2018 Macron's government announced the fuel tax hike was put on hold and promised an increase in minimum wage and tax-free overtime payments and bonuses. Macron refused to reinstate the wealth tax but agreed to increase the property tax. Despite France ranking highest among OECD countries in public social spending, it is beset with economic and social problems.

Euro Health-Care

Let's turn to progressive demands in the US. AOC admits to the coercive elements in her socialist agenda. Not so the Chair of the Democratic National Committee, **Tom Perez**, who, when asked on "Fox News Sunday" (2/24/19) how he defends against Trump's charged that the Democratic Party is now socialist, recalled how President Ronald Reagan would call everything "socialist" as a scare tactic— *"the oldest trick"*. These candidates are really asking, he said, *"How do we make sure America works for everyone?"* But socialism by any other name smells just as bad. To quote James Lileks ("Athwart," *NR*, 3/11/19): "*if something looks like a duck, quacks like a duck, and advocates total government control over the nation's economy like a duck, it is indeed a duck, and probably one with an M.A. from Columbia.*"

NR's Kevin Williamson addresses the misconception of some progressives that Europe's health-care system enjoys a centralized government apparatus and that private insurance has been outlawed. While the left sees its proposals for a federal health-care system as "British," progressives are really talking about a Soviet system since the Brits haven't abolished private insurance as Senator Kamala Harris proposes. The Medicare-for-all agenda endorsed by Democratic Senators Harris, Bernie Sanders, Elizabeth Warren, and Kirsten Gillibrand would cost $3.5 trillion a year, more than all tax revenue for 2018. The defects of this model are everywhere including the UK and Canada, "*where delays, poor quality of care, and corruption are ongoing problems that are getting worse*" (2/25/19). Very few countries, he writes, "*have a single, unitary, national-monopoly system of the kind Democrats are envisioning*"—no single-payer system in Germany or France. Sweden has a decentralized system in which care lies with county governments or municipalities. Switzerland relies upon private insurance and emphasizes "*cross-jurisdictional competition, consumer choice, and individual responsibility.*"

Scandinavia—Denmark, Sweden, Norway, and Finland—are not Nordic socialist countries--they have no mandated minimum wage or guaranteed jobs. They bear a heavy tax burden paid for by the middle and working classes largely through the Value-Added-Tax on goods—that's a consumption tax (like congestion pricing), not a tax on income (which they have) nor on wealth. The Danish PM Lars-Lokke Rasmussen himself rejects the socialist label: "*Denmark is far from a socialist planned economy. Denmark is a market economy.*"

So is Sweden. To speak of Sweden is no longer to speak of a culturally homogeneous Nordic paradise of Germanic roots. Although Bernie Sanders and his ilk continue to present it as an ideal socialist state, in reality, Sweden is a generous liberal welfare state that has had to privatize, deregulate, and rollback some of its perks and that enjoys a robust market economy.

Unlike socialist Cuba or Venezuela, Sweden is a constitutional monarchy run by a freely elected parliament and prime minister with an independent judiciary. Local governments, not the central government, control most of the public sector and their own tax base. The public service sector is large, with about 1/3 of the workforce paid by taxpayer revenue. Yes, its social welfare system provides universal healthcare. Here's a surprise: Sweden is a world leader in private pensions. It supports both public and private college education. How? Taxes. Today there is a 2-tiered progressive income tax (municipal and high-income state tax), payroll taxes, and the ubiquitous VAT taxes.

From 1970 to 1990 taxes in Sweden grew by more than 10% while economic growth stalled. The fiscal crisis in the 1990s led to governmental reduced welfare state benefits and privatization of many public services and goods. Taxes have been dropping since 1990, with taxes for the highest earners dropping the most. In 1990, 52.3% of GDP was collected as taxes. In 2006, total tax revenue was 49.1% of GDP; it dropped to 47.8% in 2007, the 2nd highest tax burden among industrialized countries. In 2010, 45.8% of GDP was collected as taxes, nearly double the percentage of that in the US. A 2012 OECD report indicated that Sweden ranked 2nd highest in public social spending (as a percentage of GDP) after France. Still, among developed nations, Sweden is no longer the highest tax country. Denmark has that privilege and has a larger public sector (38%) of the workforce than Sweden.

Concurrent with its economic growth and surge in immigration has been a growth in "inequality" and social unrest that have been attributed by the Left to cutbacks in government benefits and the trend toward privatization of public services. The riots in May 2013 in a suburb of Sweden by Muslim youth, reported by Andrew Higgens in the *New York Times* (5/26/13), left visiting American social workers perplexed on seeing the well-maintained public housing: *"It's green and safe, so what is the problem?"* Rioters burned cars and threw stones at arriving firemen. An OECD report said income inequality had grown faster in Sweden than in any other industrialized nation since 1985 (although far more equal than most). Yet immigrant suburbs, including Husby, where the riots began on May 19, 2013, after police fatally shot a 69-year-old Portuguese immigrant wielding a knife, *"show few outward signs of deprivation"*—with youth centers, libraries, and social workers *"financed by the state,"* wrote scholar and blogger Horace Jeffrey Hodges

("Stockholm: What's the Problem?" 6/12/13).

"The rich are getting richer, and the poor are getting poorer," said an activist in the opposition Left Party at the time, Barbro Sorman, adding, *"Sweden is starting to look like the USA,"* evoking both the poet Shelley and Bernie Sanders. Perhaps, hordes of unskilled and unassimilated immigrant laborers are the problem.

Sweden has a highly skilled, export-oriented manufacturing sector. It may surprise AOC that the overwhelming majority of Swedish industry is privately controlled—even the energy industry is largely privatized. Sweden has a lower corporate tax rate than the US (*NYT*, 3/9/19). Out of those 10 million residents, 4.5 million are employed. In 2017 the unemployment rate was 7.2%, but youth unemployment has been much higher.

The influx of Muslim migrants and refugees in Sweden has upset the social and economic balance. In 2009, Israel's Davis Cup team played its matches in Sweden in an empty stadium because the Swedes couldn't guarantee safety from the mobs, noted Charles Krauthammer (*Washington Post*, 1/10/14). It is now subject to violent gang shootings and other crime in the suburbs of Stockholm. This once most egalitarian of nations has in its modern midst pockets of Muslim immigrants where the subjugation of women is a cultural and religious fact of life (see *Hate Crimes: Who's to Blame?"*). Signs of Muslim fundamentalism are evident in the Rinkeby neighborhood of Stockholm, where young girls wear headscarves and stores sell hijabs and face veils, in Tensta, another one of Sweden's 23 *"extremely vulnerable district,"* where leftwing posters feature Muslims, and in nearby Alby, where a leftist political party plays Arabic music, reports *NR's* Andy Ng (12/31/18). From 2012 to 2015, 300 Swedish nationals, 70% from "vulnerable" neighborhoods, traveled to the Middle East to join Islamist groups. Another 2000 are on the government's radar as potential jihadists. In April 2017, an Uzbek *"failed asylum seeker,"* an ISIS supporter who'd lived in Tensta, drove through a busy Stockholm street, killing 5 and injuring 14.

By 2013, 15% of the population was foreign-born and another 15% were born to 2 immigrant parents. Sweden accepted more than 160,000 asylum-seekers in 2015, nearly 2% of its total population, and nearly 40,000 in October alone. During the European migrant crisis of 2015, thousands of migrants and asylum seekers arrived from Africa and the Middle East, with

Sweden admitting the most migrants per capita —mostly young men, writes Ngo. The country known by American socialists for its welfare benefits is now also known "*for gang shootings, grenade attacks and sexual crimes.*" Billions have been spent on resettling asylum seekers from disparate cultures. Within one generation, "*Sweden has experienced a dramatic demographic transformation.*" Immigrant neighborhoods now line the southern city of Malmo, where Ngo stopped at the Malmo Synagogue enclosed in a metal security fence and closed-circuit cameras. The synagogue was attacked with explosives in 2010 and in December 2017, after Trump recognized Jerusalem as Israel's capital, it was where hundreds of protestors called for an intifada and promised to "*shoot the Jews.*" Notes Ngo: "*One of the consequences of mass migration to Europe that no one had predicted was the importation of a different strain of anti-Semitism.*"

The foreign-born made up 18% of the population by 2016, double that of 1990, reported Rich Lowry in the *Post* (2/22/17), so that Sweden "*has now clamped down on its borders.*" Since 2015, most immigrants hail from Syria, neighboring Finland, and Iraq (also from Poland, Iran and Somalia). There is a wide gap in labor-participation between native Swedes (82%) and foreign-born (57%), encouraged by welfare state support, and Sweden spends more on asylum-seekers than national defense (3/22/17). In a country of more than 10 million residents (10,223,505 in 2018), in 2017, Statistic Sweden estimated more than 3 million, some 31.5% of Swedes, had a foreign background—they were born abroad or were born in Sweden with at least 1 parent born abroad.

Sweden's 8% Muslim population in 2016 would skyrocket to 31% in a high migration scenario by 2050 (compared to 21% in the medium migration scenario and 11% in the zero Muslim migration), according to demographic projections by the Pew Center (see *Hate Crimes*).

The increased Muslim population has been associated with increased violence, hate crimes, and gangs. In 2005, Sweden had higher crime rates than other EU countries. Since 2014, there have been increased incidents of fraud, property crimes, and sexual offenses.

In 2010, the rapidly swelling ranks of the Sweden Democrats, an anti-immigrant rightwing party critical of Islam, lead to seats in the Riksdag. Three leftist parties won the most seats in the 2014 election, but the Sweden Democrats made gains as well. Rightwing political parties have benefitted from the demographic upheaval in Sweden as in Germany, France, and elsewhere. In 2018 the Sweden Democrats catapulted to 3rd place in September's national election, capturing nearly 18% of the vote.

With Russia as a neighbor, peaceful Sweden has had to reinstate the draft. The first recruits were to begin basic training in 2018. Reconsidering moving to Sweden? Still, those Scandinavian nations rank high on the "World Happiness Report" on 156 countries: number one is Finland, followed by Denmark, Norway and Iceland; within the top 10 (rated on wealth, life expectancy, social support, and other factors) is Sweden.

Feds Are Forever

50 years ago, if you worked for Bulova in your twenties, you probably worked for Bulova when you retired (and got a gold watch). There's been rapid job turnover in the US for decades. With the advent of managed care, doctors began joining group and hospital practices. The internet changed the world. Amazon knocked out retail stores, and robots knocked out unskilled laborers. High corporate taxes sent manufacturing jobs overseas. Who had job security? The highly skilled if they could change with the new demands, and of course federal employees.

In the US the federal employee is untouchable. If you're a New Yorker who rarely gets your mail on time, come the holiday season you're lucky if you get it at all, when piles of mail are dumped into the trash by postal workers unloading the overload. Yet you never hear of a mailman being fired. Retired postal workers talk of the ineptness, the laziness, and the theft by other postal employees of promising looking packages, such as oversized "talking" congratulatory or commiserative greetings cards that are pulled off the line because they might contain a cash gift. You hear about the failing, debt-ridden USPS and increases in the cost of stamps but never about measures to improve service or to diminish postal crime. Such is the world of job security. Recently, a certified letter sent by a friend failed to reach its destination after several weeks. The post office blamed a postal distribution center in Manhattan and stopped replying to inquiries. In another case, an item ordered online was to be delivered in Manhattan by USPS and was sent priority mail, overnight delivery. USPS texted it would arrive between 8 AM – 8 PM. It did arrive—after 8 PM.

After a White House employee in February 2019 leaked the president's schedule to the media, Acting Chief of Staff Mick Mulvaney told Chris Wallace ("Fox News Sunday," 2/10/19) that when they pinpoint the culprit it will be difficult to fire him or her; he also said many employees were not hired by this administration.

Margaret Thatcher famously declared that the reason socialism fails is that it runs out of other people's money. Here in the States in the post-FDR era, we have a safety net for the individual and government subsidies for select industries—combo crony capitalism and bailouts for too-big-to-fail industries. Under President Obama, the Democratic Party pushed a vision of "Julia," a fictitious character—naturally, a woman given her dependency— who receives cradle-to-grave benefits à la Sweden including child-care.

The socialist march began in the 2016 election with Senator Bernie Sanders, an avowed socialist who served as an independent in the Senate but caucused with Democrats. He's in the race again for 2020. Elizabeth Warren won't bother with puny tax hikes; she says as president she'd confiscate wealth in huge bites and redistribute it. You've got 3 homes. Not anymore under Liz.

A *New York Post* columnist born in the former Soviet Union writes that the Young Democratic Socialists of America website disassociates its economic program from the Soviet failure yet their ideas *"aren't much different from those that formed the basis for that failed state: 'from each according to his ability to each according to his need'"* (NYP, 8/6/18). Karol Markowicz knows *"about the transfer of private industry to government control"*: her grandfather's father had his bakery seized in Gomel, and he was sent to a gulag, where he died.

"What happens when the state runs out of money from the industries seized and needs more?" asks Markowicz (8/6/18). It's funny how socialism-lovers *"dismiss the underlying foundation in countries that have veered toward some form of that system: capitalism,"* writes Markowicz. She cites Norway as an example, helped by an abundance of natural resources, *"an essentially capitalist system supporting the welfare state."* The hard-left resents even nominal US intervention in Venezuela, a failed socialist state. Venezuela has abundant resources as well. It was a thriving country until it fell under the dictatorship of Hugo Chavez in 1999, and that of Nicholas Maduro since 2013. People are starving under this socialist regime although the country remains the world's number 1 oil

producer.

President Trump addressed the dire situation in Venezuela in the largest Venezuelan community in the US—at Florida International University in Miami—on February 18th. *"There's nothing less Democratic than socialism, which always gives rise to tyranny,"* he said at the rally in support of opposition leader Juan Guaido, recognized as president by the US, EU, much of Latin America, and other nations following the sham reelection of Nicolas Maduro, described by Trump as a *"man controlled by the Cuban military and a private army of Cuban soldiers".* Socialism is a *"failed ideology"* that *"shut down free markets, repressed free speech,"* and *"destroyed the rule of law."*

Cuba is now a cheap attraction for American tourists. You don't hear about the prisons. Cuba remains a single-party socialist system and centrally planned economy, one of the world's last communist holdouts, with an unstable economy and rigged "elections" such as on a new constitution.

If I Were A Rich Man

People rage against the exorbitant salaries of CEOs. They are usually unaware of the outsized salaries of university presidents. They fully accept the million-dollar packages given to sports team players, network TV anchors, and successful actors who preach social justice but donate a pittance of their wealth to charity.

China has its own version of a Forbes rich list called the Hurun Report. Following the 2018 stock market dive, Chinese billionaires still outnumbered those from any other country as of January 31st. 658 billionaires enjoy the Communist dictatorship while 212 entrepreneurs lost billionaire status.

The US has 584 billionaires (and Germany 117). The Forbes billionaires list, writes Kevin Williamson, contains *"some of the best evidence there is against the argument one hears from Senator Sanders et. al. that the United States is an oligarchy characterized by hereditary privilege and corporate hoarding. Two of the remarkable absences from the list: heirs and CEOs"* (NR, 4/2/18). Bernie Sanders might not know that *"there's nobody in the top ten who simply inherited and husbanded a fortune, and very few elsewhere."* Williamson wrote this article before New York bumbled the Amazon deal and before the Bezos's sexting fiasco put his fortune at risk. But it's been well known that Bezos came from humble roots-- the son of a teenaged mom, who following marriage to his father married a Cuban immigrant and moved to Houston, where Bezos attended public schools. Later came Princeton and entrepreneurship.

The Forbes list is chock full of CEOs who mostly made their money not as executives but as business founders, such as Microsoft's Bill Gates, Steve Ballmer, and Paul Allen. Williamson makes a nifty comparison between current Microsoft CEO Satya Nadella, who is not on the list's top 1,000, and vodka entrepreneur Bert "Tito" Beveridge (everyone's given up Grey Goose for Tito), who is twice as rich. *"There's a lesson in that: If you want to fly around on someone else's jet, be a CEO. If you want to fly around on your own jet, start the company."* Williamson offers another lesson: none of the philanthropy by the Walton heirs has done as much good *"for ordinary people—and for poor people—as Walmart itself,"* the retail megastore despised by progressives that *"has done more to transfer wealth from the shareholder class to the poor than every tweedy Piketty-quoting intellectual in the Western world combined."* The top 10 Americans on the list are associated with fairly new companies—Facebook (2004), Google (1998), Amazon (1994). Bezos is now the richest man in the world. Facebook has more than 2 billion monthly active users!

Most of us pay into the safety net of Social Security, Medicare, and unemployment insurance, many of us are eligible to partake of government largesse in the form of welfare, Medicaid, child-care programs (such as Head Start) and the Child Tax Credit. Medicare, Medicaid, and Social Security account for half of all federal spending. Most of us have witnessed both Democrats and Republicans promote corporate bailouts, corporate welfare, and crony capitalism--failed solar company Solyndra received $535 million in the stimulus package during the Obama administration.

In dismissing Amazon, AOC talked about *"corporate greed."* She is both ignorant and a hard woman to please. Thronged at the South by Southwest festival in Austin, Texas, on March 10th, she knocked FDR's original New Deal as *"an extremely economically racist policy that drew little red lines around black and brown communities, and it invested in white America."* "Redlining" was an illegal practice that began in the 1930s linked to the federal Home Owners' Loan Corp. in which minorities were not shown properties or offered mortgage loans, giving whites *"access to the greatest source of intergenerational wealth."* AOC trashed Ronald Reagan for allegedly pitting the white working class against blacks and Hispanics. This is what she thinks of *"where we are"* today: *"And this idea of like 10 percent better from garbage shouldn't be what we settle for."* Perhaps, she should see the world.

The left-behind include the neglected homeless population, the unemployed, and uneducated, unskilled workers. JPMorgan Chase CEO Jamie Dimon focused on the *"Forty percent of Americans"* who make less than $15/hour, the *"Fifteen percent of Americans make minimum wages"* on March 18th, while unveiling a job-training program. He did not break down the numbers into how many were upwardly mobile youngsters who would one day complete high school or college and move up the pay scale.

The formula for individual success is not cradle-to-grave benefits. According to a 2017 Institute for Family Studies and American Enterprise Institute study, 71% of even low-income millennials who follow the "success sequence"—finish high school, get married, and then have kids—will attain the *"middle or higher end of the income distribution by the time they are age 28 – 34,"* reports David French (*NR*, 2/25/19). The late New York senator Daniel Patrick Moynihan addressed our social problems decades ago. Although he remains a liberal icon, liberals didn't always like his answers. The answers today lie in part in our broken families, broken schools, dis-incentivized unemployed adults, fraying common civic fabric, and toxic political climate. Not in class-warfare or identity politics.

3 GIMME STATUS

"Bart's out of the picture, Mr. Lavery. For the time—"
"Doctor. It's Dr. Lavery." He lowered himself into an armchair and we sat opposite him.
"You got a stethoscope, a prescription pad, and a license to practice medicine, then I'll call you 'doctor.' Every other 'ologist' who writes a dissertation on some useless theoretical load of crap is just plain old 'mister' to me."—Fictional NYPD Homicide Detective Mike Chapman addressing an academic in anthropology in *The Dead House* by Linda Fairstein (2001)

In *Faux Equality* and other books, I have written about the desire of equal status for unequal qualifications. Under that rubric we might put psychologists wanting prescribing privileges without going to medical school, "health-care providers" wanting the same privileges and pay as physicians. Wrote a professor of surgery: *'In my 40-year career, our devaluation has been a slow and painful process. It started with being called a 'provider.' This devalues me. Call me by what I am and do. Physician. Doctor. That is what our patients call us'* (Bhagwan Satiani, MD, *Clinical Psychiatry News*, Feb. 2019).

So many self-proclaimed experts. Technicians who pass themselves off as licensed electricians. Talking heads on TV who only yesterday were political hacks now claim to be foreign affairs or national security mavens. Academics in fields without genuine scholarship who want to be taken seriously. Administrators who seek to punish those who mock the grievance-industry by submitting bogus papers to social science journals (see *Hate Crimes*).

Workers and business people complain that millennials say they want a job but don't want to work. They don't want to follow orders. They talk in trendy terms without understanding their meaning. They live on social media, where they get their news in short sound-bites. They want a fancy title before acquiring expertise. In January 2019 Anne Helen Petersen's essay "Millennial Burnout" described how they find their identity in a job and feel work should never end, notes Karol Markowicz (*NYP*, 3/18/19): "*things that should've felt bad (working all the time) felt good, because I was doing what I thought I should and needed to be doing in order to succeed,*" wrote Petersen. Yet, bosses complain about millennials as do colleagues, merchants, and salesmen that cater to their needs.

Titles are nice but too often they go to people's heads and they forget yours. Or, if they're politicians, they believe their title—whether an elected position or by appointment—entitles them to ignore the rules but chastise others who also bend the rules. There's AOC who thinks she can talk the talk about green energy but walk the walk of the rest of us, taking planes and cabs to save time. There's Mayor de Blasio who thanks the Supreme Court for its narrow definition of public corruption. He can continue to violate the public trust with impunity. So can his wife whose political aspirations led to her being in charge of a mental health initiative. How did she qualify for this position? Her marital status. We need not mention the FBI renegades, former FBI Director James Comey and Acting Director Andrew McCabe. They'll get theirs in a later chapter.

Status is a marketable asset. It also inspires self-confidence. Piles of money enhance status whether it's earned legally, or honestly, whether it's related to one's talents or to being famous for being famous. Money can dictate our health-care choices. Growing up rich may provide a better indicator for making healthy choices than later wealth when, even if you're a president, you're addicted to fast food. Just ask Bill Clinton or his cardiologists.

Harvard professor and physician Andrew A. Nierenberg wrote: "*Our socioeconomic status should not matter, especially when it comes to health. And yet it does. We can predict your health and life expectancy from your zip code! The social determinants of health are profound*" (*Psychiatric Annals*, March 2018). In a study of British civil servants, those in higher status jobs had better health and lived longer, highlighting the importance of self-worth, Nierenberg writes. The effects of chronic stress are various, none of them good.

The list of top-rated ZIP codes in the US has some surprises. Florida has 3 in the top 10, but I was surprised to see Fisher Island (where Oprah and Mel Brooks have homes) off Miami as number one (Palm Beach only made number 4 and Boca Grande came in nine). New York State has 2 listings on the top 10. A surprise: Tribeca's made it to number five, up from only number 22 last year. I know some lawyers and a physician who bought more 20 years ago, when it was still largely commercial. Harrison, New York in Westchester placed sixth. Also, in the top 10 are 3 addresses in California (Atherton, Palo Alto, and Century City). In 2019, New York City lost title to being the most popular city in the world for the rich, surpassed by London, according to the 2019 Douglas Elliman Knight Frank Wealth Index Report. New York still has the highest number of billionaires—94. In 2018, San Francisco and Chicago made the top 5 (at 3 and 5 respectively), but not in 2019. LA dropped a notch, from 4 in 2018 to 5 this year.

There is one profession I have followed for its widespread unprofessionalism: journalism. There was a time when famous journalists had a high school education. Brian Williams didn't graduate college. These high school graduates knew how to investigate, to get the who, what, when, where, and how of a story. They knew how to write; some even had a flair. Later came journalism schools for the upwardly mobile "journalist". Later still came the pretentiousness of journalism. The media revel in the use of "experts." Everyone is an expert today whether in a frequently imprecise field such as polling or meteorology or in an esoteric offshoot of a familiar field. Some experts have bona fide credentials and experience in their fields, such as Dr. Oz or former judge Andrew Napolitano. Sometimes journalists become the experts—such as on panels for discussion on cable TV.

Journalism used to be a craft, a vocation. Talent helps. As print newspapers have declined in numbers and readership, as online news sites have proliferated, as bloggers offer contradictions and rebuttals to what has been called the "mainstream media," the lines have blurred between professional "journalists" and non-professionals.

The public distrusts the media as much as it distrusts Congress. News media—particularly the *New York Times*, CNN, MSNBC—have great difficulty separating news from opinion. "Gimme the news straight" –a cry from the public—will not get these left-wing organizations to deliver the news straight up. You'll get opinion journalism on Fox News, but it's usually confined to opinion show anchors such as Tucker Carlson or Sean Hannity or Laura Ingraham. That's where it should be. If you want the news straight, watch Fox News's evening news programs—Brett Baier's "Special Report" or Martha MacCallum's "The Story." Chris Wallace presents both sides of an issue on "Fox News Sunday" but usually skewers Republicans and treads lightly with Democrats. Someone fairer and talented and younger may one day give Wallace a run for his money—that's Harris Faulkner, the host of the midday news show, "Outnumbered Overtime." You can't separate news from opinion in *The New York Times* or on CNN or MSNBC. After the release of the Mueller report, ratings of MSNBC's fibbing newscasters plummeted.

Recently, Ted Koppel criticized the liberal bias of mainstream media, particularly the anti-Trump *New York Times* and *Washington Post*. **Jill Abramson**, a former editor of the *Times*, wrote about that newspaper's bias towards Trump. Nearly all news reports about him—whether during the election period or after his victory—have been negative. They have been the source of frequent leaks that seemed to point to a smoking gun revelation regarding collusion, obstruction of justice, or criminal activity, only to put the weapon back in its holster later in the piece.

Lara Logan, a former "60 Minutes" correspondent said on a podcast, "Mike Drop," in February 2019 that too many in the media have become "*political activists*" who stray from journalistic standards and display obvious bias. She then wrote a piece for *The New York Post* (2/27/19), "*Truth – our one & only job.*"

"*There is nothing more human than opinions and bias. To say we have none is dishonest. But what we do have as professional journalists is a simple standard to get us past that: two firsthand sources—question everything and independently verify.*" That's Logan's creed that she inherited from Edward R. Murrow. "*Journalists are not activists,*" she proclaims although that's obviously not true today when journalists don't follow the facts wherever they lead, but like corrupt FBI agents, create facts to alter a situation they deplore. "*Nor are we lawyers in a court of law, cherry-picking facts to prove our case,*" Logan insists. That's of course how liberal journalists justify the executive overreach of Obama while blasting every executive order by Trump. *"Above all, we are not propagandists or political operatives. That is not our job."* The leaks by the *Times* moments after Trump was inaugurated were geared to undermining his presidency and bolstering talk about "collusion." The *Times* and *Washington Post* had the means, but not the moral imperative, to expose the abuses of the FISA court and the abuses by high-ranking officials in the FBI and DOJ who were engaged in effecting a bureaucratic coup.

To be a journalist today is to be a presumptive liar. Logan puts it differently: *"Everywhere I go, people tell me they have lost faith in journalism."* Fact: *"the vast majority of journalists in this country are registered Democrats. The colleges we come from are similarly dominated by one political ideology. This matters today because the reporting has become so one-sided."* She goes on to mention that many journalists claiming to be objective have taken a political stand, *"saying the urgency of the time justifies a departure from journalistic standards."* As examples, Logan mentions *Time* magazine falsely reporting on Trump's first day in office, stating he'd removed the bust of Martin Luther King from the Oval Office. She reports that there are 70 other examples on a list compiled by investigative reporter Sharyl Attkisson.

Logan reports that *"propaganda machines like David Brock and his staff at Media Matters for America smear, manipulate and invent false narratives driven by their well-funded political agenda."* With a stable of journalists, *"they silence and intimidate."* They turn reports of bias by independent journalists into false accusations of being conservative, clearly a dirty word in the big business of journalism.

Part of the problem is not just bias among reporters. It's a notion that, somehow, they are part of an elite esprit de corps, they offer expertise, an insight that is sharper than their readers', and so, they cannot, must not, report the news without informing stupid readers what they should think. So, we have leading reporters and journalists that are both biased and supercilious. Their knowledge-base is often shoddy. Their college curriculum was heavy on squish and light on rigorous courses. There are few journalists who reach the stature of the late great Dr. Charles Krauthammer or former academic and *Washington Post* syndicated columnist George Will.

Another part of the problem is that on TV—whether network or cable—the anchor has to be engaging, personable, and magnetic to keep viewers' attention. In other words, he or she must be somewhat of an actor. Bill O'Reilly, a not very astute anchor, was usually sufficiently dramatic and nasty to guests to keep his audience riveted. He had the number one show on Fox News, higher ratings than the infinitely more interesting and intelligent anchor, Chris Wallace of "Fox News Sunday."

Several of the TV network stars inflate their worth with tall-tales about themselves or political leaders they detest. In a piece on our shameless society—think Lt. Gov. of Virginia Justin Fairfax still in office despite accusations of sexual assault, former President Bill Clinton and his sexual exploits—Maureen Callahan points out two prominent figures in journalism. Former *New York Times* editor Jill Abramson was *"called out for plagiarizing at least six passages in her book about the state of journalism – which she denied before admitting to making 'mistakes' that nonetheless should not 'overshadow what I think is a really interesting book',"* and *"Congenital liar Brian Williams still anchors a nightly newscast."*

A "Page Six" item (3/1/19) --"Lyin' Brian back from brink?" -- speculates that **Brian Williams** could come back from exile. The world-renowned anchor was booted from "NBC Nightly News" in 2015 after it was revealed he'd embellished some stories with fictional details—and sent to the Siberia of 11 PM on sister station MSNBC. Despite his tarnished rep, Williams made his "11th Hour with Brian Williams" a legit hit, proclaims the gossip page, beating CNN and Fox News for 3 straight months. Insiders say Williams could replace Chris Matthews ("Hardball") at 7 PM, and there are industry rumors that network bosses are unimpressed with Chuck Todd's "Meet the Press" spinoff "MTP Daily."

Lying Brian didn't have fancy credentials. To be a good newsman, he didn't need to graduate from Columbia's School of Journalism—at least in his time. It did help to be diligent, articulate, and honest. Two out of three turned out to be bad. The Jersey boy who graduated from a parochial high school but never stuck through George Washington University made his way up the NBC News ladder. He covered the Iraq War in 2003. With Williams on board the NBC Nightly News in December 2004, the network won the Peabody Award for coverage of Hurricane Katrina and Williams accepted the award. In 2007 *Time* magazine named him one of the 100 most influential people in the world. In 2009, he won the Walter Cronkite Award for

Excellence in Journalism.

In February 2015, Williams fell from glory despite his $10 million a year salary and 5-year contract that was signed in 2014. He was suspended for 6 months without pay and then demoted from the Nightly News for misrepresenting *"events which occurred while he was covering the Iraq War in 2003."* On February 4th, he recanted the story he'd told on a January 30th broadcast claiming the military helicopter he'd been on had been *"forced down after being hit by an RPG."* The story had been disproven: another helicopter had been forced to make an emergency landing, while Brian's arrived somewhere between a half-hour to an hour later. His original report on 3/26/03 noted that *"the Chinook ahead of us was almost blown out of the sky."* In 2007 his reference to the incident was that an RPG *"that had been fired at us, and it hit the chopper in front of us."* By 2013 Williams said his helicopter had been *"hit"* and *"landed very quickly."*

It's fun to be a hero, and Williams' tendency to embellish his adventures became evident with scrutiny. He had talked about flying into Baghdad with Navy SEAL Team Six, but SEALs don't embed journalists. Williams had claimed in 2014 that *"We watched, all of us watched, as one man committed suicide"* at the New Orleans Superdome in the aftermath of Hurricane Katrina in 2005. He had not been a witness. In 2006 he told *The Daily Show* with Jon Stewart that he'd nearly been hit while riding an Israeli Black Hawk helicopter by Katyusha rockets fired by Hezbollah from Lebanon. He screwed up on recounting the details. The helicopter had not been in danger. Williams craved the spotlight, even when danger was not involved. The Berlin Wall fell on November 9, 1989. Williams claimed in 2008 that he'd been at the Brandenburg Gate at the time. In reality, he arrived a day later, on the 10th.

Williams remained in purgatory as anchor at MSNBC. From 2016, he's also been anchor of "11th Hour". What's left open for Williams? According to Page Six, Williams won't return to one of the major evening news gigs. An NBC News source said a lot of NBC journalists *"think Brian should've lost his job. He's kind of forgotten at NBC News."* To one MSNBC source, although William's 2015 fibbing now seems *"almost quaint"* compared to #Me Too Matt Lauer and Charlie Rose, there's no current plan to move him to a different slot. However, sources said that along with Rachel Maddow, Williams will be fronting the outlet's 2020 election coverage. *"Brian's done an amazing job of keeping his head down and working,"* said a network source. *"He hasn't tried to take any victory laps at MSNBC."*

It's really more than one "fib." Williams hogs the limelight. In today's partisan coverage of the news, a discredited overpaid journalist should be kept in check. Fame and money weren't enough for Williams. He wanted glory. What motivated the lies of another famous journalist was political animus toward a political leader. Just like the "fake news" today directed at President Trump.

Dan Rather lied for ideology, not for personal glory. No great academic credentials were needed (he has a BA in journalism from Sam Houston State University and briefly attended South Texas College of Law). He climbed the ranks at CBS News: White House correspondent in 1964, foreign correspondent, White House correspondent during the Nixon era, anchor of CBS "Sunday Night News" in the 70s, correspondent for "60 Minutes," and after Walter Cronkite retired in 1981, anchor of the CBS Evening News for 24 years—one of the "Big Three" (Peter Jenkins at ABC and Tom Brokaw at NBC). His show was in 3rd place from 1992 until 2005, when Rather fell from the apex of journalism in 2005, the victim of his own hubris, after peddling unauthenticated documents in new reports on President George W. Bush's Vietnam-era service in the Texas National Guard.

"60 Minutes II" ran Rather's 2004 report about Bush's military record. Rather admitted the documents' authenticity (memos in files of Lt. Bush's former commanding officer, Lt. Col. Jerry Killian) could not be proven. Talk about forgery spread in the *New York Times* and *Washington Post*. CBS later said Texas Army National Guard Lt. Col. Bill Burkett had misled the network. CBS News retracted the story and fired multiple staffers (including story producer Mary Mapes) but kept Rather on.

There were prior cases of Rather playing fast and loose with the truth. A 2004 article by Anne Morse said almost nothing in Rather's CBS News special in 1988, "The World Within" on Vietnam, was true, with all 6 servicemen interviewed lying about their experiences.

Rather continued to work for CBS until 2006 and then for cable AXS TV, hosting "Dan Rather Reports" until 2013. In January 2018, Rather began an online newscast on The Young Turks You Tube channel. He continues to cling to righteousness: "*Nobody has proved they were fraudulent, much less a forgery,*" Rather said on "Larry King Live" in September 2007. "*The truth of this story stands up to this day.*" He filed a lawsuit against CBS and its then-parent company Viacom, for making him a "scapegoat." In 2009, the New York Court of Appeals dismissed the lawsuit. Ideologues may make good preachers, but they make lousy reporters.

After the Mueller report clearing Trump of collusion was submitted to AG Bill Barr, the *New York Post*'s Sohrab Ahmari ran a contest for #Mueller Madness among print journalists, cable talking heads, Twitter Trump haters, and network reporters. His pick for cable was MSNBC's Rachel Maddow for "*nonstop collusion rants.*" More than 1,000 readers responded, with nearly ¼ picking Maddow for the top spot. Her insights included, "*the presidency is effectively a Russian op.*" 2nd was CNN anchor Don Lemon. The winner for print journalism, sad to say, was editor-at-large of *The Bulwark*, the former editor of *The Weekly Standard*, which folded in part because of Bill Kristol's blind Never-Trump prism. Network TV winner was SNL actor Alec Baldwin. Among the Twitterati, top scorer was senior fellow at Brookings, Benjamin Wittes, and 2nd place was Harvard Law School Professor Lawrence Tribe.

4 GIMME HARVARD

"Harvard today engages in the same kind of discrimination and stereotyping that it used to justify quotas on Jewish applicants in the 1920s and 1930s."—Students for Fair Admissions

A lawsuit in Boston against Harvard for a de facto quota system that discriminates against Asian-Americans by using a "holistic" scale that consistently finds them deficient in personal qualities, and a lawsuit in New York City to stymie plans for a quota system in elite public high schools that would discriminate against high-achieving Asian students, highlight the problem with racial preferences and set-asides. These have been ongoing conflicts between high-achievers and "social justice" administrators that I've written about in *Faux Inequality* and *Due Process Undone*.

Asian-Americans Battle Harvard

If you were told a high school student was very studious, that his peers were similarly eager beavers, intent on attending an Ivy League college, and that his parents were pushing him to succeed academically, you might think he fit the Asian-American stereotype. If you were following the news regarding admission to elite colleges for the past decade (or reading my books *Faux Equality* and *Due Process Undone*), you would know that he was not a shoe-in at Harvard. Students of other races with a lower academic profile have a better chance of acceptance to America's most prestigious university. Between 1995 and 2013, Asian-American applicants had the lowest acceptance rate of any racial group (NR). This is not to say their presence is negligible. Despite the higher bar to admissions, Asians at Harvard constituted about 22% of admissions in 2017 but just 5% of the population (www.vox.com).

Why the higher bar? The story begins with a presidential executive order—that of JFK in 1961, establishing affirmative action. By the 1980s, the number of high-performing Asian-American college applicants had skyrocketed, but their percentage in the student body at elite colleges remained flat.

Until recently, the legal assault on affirmative action has been spearheaded by rejected white applicants who had a better academic profile than some minority students who were admitted. In *Regents of California v. Bakke*, the US Supreme Court (USSC) in 1977 injected the mantra of diversity. It struck down the Davis medical school admissions program that used a quota system to reject a white male applicant while admitting non-whites with lower test scores, but upheld the use of affirmative action such as that used by Harvard, which considered race as one of several factors leading to a diverse student body. Nebulous rulings continued. In 2003, in *Grutter v. Bollinger*, the USSC upheld the University of Michigan's Law School's limited use of race in admissions, which could be considered among "*all factors that may contribute to student body diversity*" that included extracurricular activities and volunteer work, approving a school's ensuring "*exposure to widely diverse people, cultures, ideas and viewpoints*," and struck down the undergraduate admissions process that gave blacks points for race at the university in *Gratz v. Bollinger*.

Abigail Fisher was rejected from the University of Texas at Austin. *Fisher* I in 2013 was sent back to a lower court to determine whether the school had shown that it had to use race to achieve diversity. Three years later in *Fisher v. Texas* (*Fisher* II) the USSC narrowly upheld the use of affirmative action only when race was, as Justice Anthony Kennedy wrote, "*a factor of a factor of a factor.*" The Texas plan, reported the *New York Times* (6/23/16), calls for automatic admission of the top 10% of Texas students, and then uses race as one of many factors regarding admissions. The University of Texas enrolled more Hispanics (19.9%) than Asians (18.6%). It considered only Hispanics to be "underrepresented," apparently because in Texas there are 3.8% Asians and 37.6% Hispanics. So, while racial quotas are verboten (*Bakke, Fisher II*) and set-asides of a fixed number or percentage that must be attained are also impermissible (*Grutter*), numerical goals, however, are permissible in which race cannot be the only or predominant factor in admissions (harvardlawreview.com).

The usefulness of demographic "diversity" as a goal—considered illegitimate by the dissent in Fisher II-- has been debated as the risks in placing under-achieving minority students in schools beyond their current capabilities became apparent. Asian-Americans found themselves in a position akin to Jewish students in the early decades of the 20th century—facing an unwritten cap at elite schools that seem to consider them socially undesirable. No matter how well they performed academically, they were not the material the Ivies wanted. Ying Ma at Fox News in October 2018 spoke of "*the sham known as diversity in higher education.*" She cited a Harvard study of applications from 2007 to 2016 that showed that using merit-based admissions, Asians would have comprised 43% of entering freshmen, not 19%. Racial diversity is "*about identity politics, and identity politics is about grievance. In turn, grievance provides an excuse for racial discrimination against different groups.*"

Edward Blum leads the Project on Fair Representation, founded in 2005 to "*support litigation that challenges racial and ethnic classifications,*" notes PR Lockhart at Vox ("The lawsuit against Harvard that could change affirmative action in college admissions," www.vox.com/2018/10/18). Blum created **Students for Fair Admissions** (SFFA), a group of anonymous Asian-American plaintiffs rejected by Harvard, which first sued the university in November 2014, alleging it was "*employing racially and ethnically discriminatory policies and procedures in administering the undergraduate admissions program*" that are biased against Asian applicants. SFFA also sued the University of North Carolina at Chapel Hill. In 2015, this coalition of 60 Asian-American groups (Chinese, Indian, Pakistani, Koreans) filed a complaint with the Department of Justice (DOJ) and Department of Education (DOE) to investigate the racial bias at Harvard.

According to the SFFA Annual Report of 2017, at Harvard in 1993, 20% of its students were Asian-Americans, and that figure has barely budged over 2 decades even as the Asian population in the US has increased rapidly. Harvard's admitted class of 2021 is 22% Asian-American, according to data on the university website. The percentage is consistent with that at Princeton and Yale.

The SFFA found that a 2013 internal Harvard study concluded that the admissions policy was discriminatory but the only action Harvard took was to conceal the report. It showed that because Asians excel on tests, grades, and extracurricular activities, Harvard routinely rates them lower on subjective categories such as "positive personality," "widely respected," "likeability," and similar categories. A male Asian-American with a 25% chance of admission would have a 35% chance if he were white, 75% if Hispanic, and 95% if black, according to the SFFA legal brief (6/18/18).

During the 15-day court proceeding, the SFFA presented reports from Harvard's Office of Institutional Research to reveal a "personal rating" process based on personal statements, teacher recommendations, and alumni interviews. Asians rank lower than whites on factors such as likability, leadership, and compassion, according to the *Washington Post*, and more whites than Asians are admitted although they rank lower on other metrics. Harvard explains that teacher recommendations account for lower personal scores for Asians. According to an analysis for SFFA by Duke economist Peter Arcidiacono that excluded from its database recruited athletes and children of alumni and faculty, Asians perform better in academic and extracurricular ratings but worse than other ethnic groups in the "personal score" and the *"magnitude of racial preferences is quite large"* (www.npr.org). Harvard's expert witness, Berkeley economist David Card, found that Asians were not less likely statistically to be admitted.

Unlike the Obama administration, whose DOE found that Princeton did not discriminate against Asians in admissions, nor use race as a deciding factor, the Trump administration in 2017 began investigating whether Harvard discriminates against Asians, and subsequently the DOJ and DOE also opened an investigation of Yale. In 2018, the Trump administration rescinded Obama-era guidelines regarding the use of race in admissions, advising colleges to adopt race-neutral procedures (www.vox.com). The DOJ filed a statement of interest with the SFFA, arguing Harvard *"failed to show that it does not unlawfully discriminate against Asian-Americans."*

The plaintiffs claim that Harvard rates Asian applicants who outperform whites academically lower on a personal scale and that it uses a quota to cap the percentage of Asian admissions in its "racial balancing" act. The trial in

Boston in October 2018—*SFFA v. Harvard*—focused on whether Harvard discriminates against Asian-Americans in violation of the Civil Rights Act, not directly on affirmative action.

The plaintiffs argued that Harvard applies 2 levels of discrimination: in recruitment and in its use of a "holistic" scale. Harvard sends recruitment letters to high school students based on standardized test scores that differ by race: Asian males in rural states must score 1370 on the PSAT to merit a letter, while white males need 1310 (Carrie Jung, "Harvard Discrimination Trial Ends, But Lawsuit Is Far From Over," www.npr.org/2018/11/02). The defense offered by the dean of admissions, William Fitzsimmons, is that the recruitment strategy is aimed at attracting rural students but those standards don't apply to the actual applicant pool. Fitzsimmons said Harvard sends recruitment letters to blacks, Native-Americans, and Hispanic high-school students with SAT scores around 1100 on math and verbal combined (out of 1600), CNN reported, while Asians receive a letter only if they score some 250 points higher—1350 for females and 1380 for males. Whites in Montana or Nevada get a letter if they have at least 1310 on their SATs. "*That's race discrimination, plain and simple,*" said SFFA lawyer John Hughes (*NYP*, 10/18/18). The dean replied, "*It is not.*"

During the trial a SFFA lawyer showed a Harvard dean who sat on committees that studied diversity and the discrimination claims bolstered by the school's 2013 study that found being Asian had a negative impact on chances of admission. Dean Rakesh Khurana had never seen it before

With relatively few black and Hispanic applicants to Harvard, Yale, and Princeton, school officials say considering race is the only means of achieving diversity. Internal reports argue that the number of black and Hispanic students would decrease if the schools changed the admissions process. The *New York Times* reported that its 2017 analysis showed that black and Hispanic students are less represented at top colleges than 35 years ago.

SFFA argues that these policies acknowledge admission of less qualified students to balance racial disparities. Harvard also argued in a pretrial filing that with nearly 40,000 applications for 2,000 spots in the class of 2019, of which more than 8,000 applicants had perfect grades, and more than 5,000 had a perfect math or verbal SAT, extracurricular activities and race must be considered in addition to test scores alone to achieve a diverse student body.

US District Court Judge Allison Burroughs is expected to release her opinion in 2019. Both sides are expected to appeal her decision. An amusing ending to the NPR piece was its advice on improving your chances of getting into Harvard: live in the sticks, donate to the school, and excel at sports; the admissions rate for recruited athletes is 80%. Jared Kushner reportedly got in after his father donated $2.5 million to Harvard. There's another means of entry to some top schools, but not Harvard: the "backdoor."

"We're not talking about donating a building so a school is more likely to take your son or daughter," proclaimed Massachusetts US Attorney Andrew Lelling when 10-month "Operation Varsity Blues" broke. *"We're talking about deception and fraud. Fake test scores. Fake athletic credentials. Fake photographs. Bribed college officials."* College prep expert, William Singer, had students posing as athletes apply as recruits in sports they never played. He gamed the system in other ways from 2011 to 2018—having a student pretend to have a disability to get more time to take the SATs, then changing the exam location to one of two test centers he controlled (West Hollywood and Houston)—and old-fashioned bribery of coaches, proctors, and 2 college-entrance-exam administrators to permit Mark Riddell to take or doctor a student's ACTs and SATs. He padded kids' résumés and passed off some as eligible for affirmative action. Students fraudulently got into Yale, Stanford, Georgetown, UCLA, USA, and other top schools. 50 people—including 33 parents and 13 coaches—were arrested on March 12th. Singer put some $25 million from parents—the average payoff was between $250,000-$400,000-- into a dummy nonprofit, his money-laundering bribery bank. Among parents facing federal charges of conspiracy to commit mail fraud and honest-services fraud are TV actresses Felicity Huffman and Lori Loughlin, co-chair of the Willkie Farr & Gallagher law firm, Gordon Caplan, CEOS, and other big names.

Deleting the Elite in New York City

Curtailing the Asian edge in academic achievement is a goal in New York City's plan to gut elite high schools to further admissions for blacks and Hispanics. The mayor and his school chancellor want to discard the use of a single objective admissions test to the Bronx High School of Science, Stuyvesant High School, and Brooklyn Technical High School and 5 other selective schools. This proposal pits one ethnic minority against two others.

In 1973 New York State passed the Hecht-Calandra bill, which required that admission to the top 3 high schools be based solely on the **Specialized High School Admissions Test**. Today 8 high-performing schools use the test, applying different cutoff points. Blacks and Hispanics make up 10% of the student body but 67% of the New York public school system. Asians from poor immigrant families make up the largest ethnic group today, just as Jews of immigrant parents did in the 1960s.

In the 2017- 2018 academic year, 73.5% of **Stuyvesant** students were Asian, nearly 18% white, 2.8% Latino, and 0.7% black, with about 44% of the student body of 3,336 living in poverty (according to DOE data on the current population of the elite 8 schools published by the *Post*, 6/4/18). **Bronx Science** with nearly 3,000 students, 44% living in poverty, had 65.6% Asians, 23.3% whites, 6.2% Hispanics, and 2.5% blacks. **Brooklyn Tech**, with over 5,800 students, nearly 61% living in poverty, had 61.3% Asians, 23.3% whites, 7.1% Hispanics, and 6.4% blacks.

The remaining 5 elite schools are Staten Island Tech, Brooklyn Latin School, the HS for Math, Science and Engineering at City College, Queens HS for the Sciences, and the HS of American Studies in the Bronx. Of these only Staten Island Tech has more than one thousand students. In four schools, Asians make up the largest cohort, with Asians comprising 81% at Queens HS for the Sciences; at American Studies nearly 60% are white.

Writes the head of the Brooklyn Tech Alumni Foundation, Larry Carry, the solution *"isn't to kill the test,"* but to *"improve the quality of education offered in African American and Latino communities from pre-K onward"* (*NYP*, 5/17/18).

That's not **Richard Carranza**'s plan. The new chancellor, a Mexican-American import from California who de Blasio describes as focused on *"social justice,"* wants to implement a quota of Hispanic and black students, regardless of how prepared these students are for the highly competitive high schools. Rather than fix the city's ailing public schools which service most minority students, Mayor de Blasio and his new school chancellor are pitching a diversity plan that would affect only a few minority students but diminish the standing of the city's premier schools. Dissenters to this plan—including Asian parents--are branded "racists." Dumping on the better high schools and fighting successful charter schools, the mayor is once again stifling education opportunities and dumbing down standards in the name of racial parity. An effort to bridge the achievement gap between black and Hispanic students and whites and Asians at the K-8 level would irk de Blasio's cash-cow ally, the corrupt teachers' union. A lawsuit against the city by Asian groups is taking on this misguided "progressive" faux egalitarianism.

Mayor **de Blasio** joins his chancellor in advocating replacing the elite high school single standard test of English, logic, and math with grades, class standing, interviews and other subjective measures. His beef is that in a school system that is roughly 70% black and Hispanic, Asians, who comprise 16% of the population, have constituted more than 60% of elite schools' student bodies.

By June 2018 the "social justice" proposal for ethnic quotas entailed set-asides for the top 7% of each of the city's 600 middle schools, many of which don't report even one student at grade level in reading or math, notes senior fellow at the Independent Women's Forum, Lisa Schiffren, a Bronx Science graduate. The plan to diversify the elite high schools got past the state Assembly's Education Committee in June.

The admissions test, de Blasio explained, would be phased out over 3 years, with 90-95% of the seats reserved for the top 7% of seventh-graders from each middle school based on a "composite score" of grades and standardized test scores. The remaining spots would be distributed via lottery to students from religious and private schools and students *"with a minimum grade-point average who are not in the top 7 percent pool."* This formula is expected to raise the total proportion of blacks and Hispanics from 9% to 45%. The mayor plans to expand the Discovery program to reserve some 1,000 seats (1/5th of the total) at the top schools for affirmative-action placement, to benefit "economically disadvantaged" kids who fall just below the cutoff. But what about the kid who is 3 points short on the exam of making it to Staten Island Tech but 50 points below the cutoff for Stuyvesant? asks the *New York Post*. This expansion of Discovery would reserve slots for areas *"with average incomes that just happen to be above the levels of most Asian 'hoods,"* notes an editorial (3/2/19), *"when the average city Asian-American income is well below median."* De Blasio chooses not to create more elite high schools unlike then-Mayor Michael Bloomberg, who added 5 to supplement the "big three."

Remedial classes eat resources, high level courses would disappear under the new plan because of the lack of qualified students, and the "meritocratic ethos" will be destroyed, warns Schiffren, who attended a college-interview event at Bronx Science where she met a Chinese student with no extra-curriculars who burst into tears as she explained that she had to work because she lived alone with her old granny. She was acing calculus, AP Latin, and chemistry. She got a full ride to college. Schiffren predicts urban flight if middle-class families lose the option of the elite high schools. She suggests leaving the top 3 alone and setting up a few borough high schools for the top 7% of middle schools.

State senator Diane Savino (D-SI), who believes "*Lowering the standards is not the way to go*," says that the state has given the city millions to offer free tutoring and test prep for the admissions test. State senator Toby Stavisky (D-Queens), a Brooklyn Tech graduate, believes the "*answer is better training for kids*," a test-prep program. By state law, only the top 3 schools have to rely on the single exam; the school chancellor could devise a plan that scraps the test for the other 5, but chooses not to do so.

The Carranza proposals would discriminate against poor Asians who account for a disproportionate number of the city's top students—the beneficiaries of the current system are East and South Asian children--and would unfairly limit the number of students from parochial and private schools. It is Asians far more than whites who are "over-represented" at top schools. Since when are impoverished Asian families considered bastions of privilege? It's not money that makes these kids high-achievers but family and personal motivation plus grit, otherwise known as studying.

A member of the Citywide Council on High Schools, Stanley Ng, explains the disparate impact the plan would have on Asian communities that are heavily concentrated in 8 of 32 school districts in Manhattan, South Brooklyn, and North Queens, whose schools are severely overcrowded. 54% of admission offers from the specialized high schools are to these 8 Asian districts (*NYP*, 2/25/19). Overall Asians make up 62% of the specialized high school student population, more than half of whom receive free or reduced-price lunches, many of whom are immigrants or the children of immigrants. The plan to "diversify" the student population by reserving the majority of seats for 7th-grade students at the top 7% of their middle school would cut the number of Asians accepted by half, according to an analysis by the city's Independent Budget Office (IBO). Limiting the number of kids from any one middle school would hurt Asian kids the most because, Ng writes, kids aged 10-12 in Brooklyn and Queens don't have access to public busses to travel to an alternative district to seek top 7% status, nor can their families afford to send them to private schools.

The new quota system for New York City's 8 top high schools would also adversely affect boys. Under the current system, the gender split is 54% male and 46% female, according to the DOE. Under the new plan, the ratio would be 62% female and 38% male, according to an IBO projection. The greater gender disparity results from new admissions criteria that include grades and classroom behavior, already used by schools that have large female majorities, such as Townsend Harris (69% female) and Beacon (64% female).

On December 3rd, some 350 Manhattan parents met with a DOE official to oppose scrapping the single admissions test to elite high schools. *"It's a political bill that's being sold on dishonest, false and even racist messaging,"* fumed a parent of 2 Stuyvesant high school students. *"Our school is not segregated. It's a loaded and racist term that they use."* Asian parents—Chinese, Korean, Bangladeshi, Pakistani—spoke of the devastating effect the quota would have on their community.

The upshot of the DOE's divide and conquer policy in late 2018 was a coalition of parents, Asian groups and schools that planned to join in a federal lawsuit to block the city's changes to specialized high school admissions. At the forefront are the parents of Intermediate School 187 in Dyker Heights, a middle school that sent the highest number of students --205--to high schools. The lawsuit is being handled by Joshua Thompson of the California-based libertarian law firm, Pacific Legal Foundation, to challenge changes to the Discovery program that allows admission to low-income applicants who fall just below the cutoff on the entry exam, changes that will intentionally lower the number of Asians admitted. Referring to the Harvard admissions case, Thompson said, *"This is becoming a major civil rights issue."* In December, Asian-Americans filed the federal lawsuit to stop the plan to reserve 20% of seats at the city's top high schools for blacks and Hispanics.

Because of the lawsuit, there was a delay in the DOE informing some 70,000 8th-graders what high school they'll attend in the fall. It announced on March 18, 2019 that 27,521 applicants took the admissions exam for the elite high schools, 4,798 secured a seat, with Asians getting 51.1% (2,450 seats), whites 28.5%%., Hispanics 6.6% (316), blacks 4.0% (190), and biracial 2.3%. The total number of seats offered through the exam was lower than in 2018 (5,057) because of the expanded Discovery program that offered more spots to low-income kids just below the test cutoff point. De Blasio reserved 11% of seats for the Discovery program, up from 5%. De Blasio, whose son attended Brooklyn Tech, still wants to increase Discovery admissions to 20% and scrap the single test that results in *"massive segregation."* Black and Hispanic enrollment declined at Brooklyn Tech, wrote Susan Edelman in the *Post*, from 51% in 1989 to almost 12% today, attributed by Tech grads to the loss since the 70s and 80s of gifted classes in elementary schools, Special Progress classes and honors and gifted programs in middle schools.

New York City's Asian community—1.3 million Asians comprise 15% of the city's population—can bolster its claim of discrimination by pointing to the negligence on the part of the ThriveNYC mental health initiative launched in 2015, the Chirlane McCray 4-year boondoggle that has not reported outcomes. Suicide is the leading cause of death of Asians in the city, higher than for other racial or ethnic groups. Asians are the poorest racial group in the city. The program doesn't fund any licensed mental-health clinics geared toward Asians (of which the city has just 3) and has no Korean-speaking staff. Awakened from slumber, Comptroller Scott Stringer on March 1st promised to examine the finances of Thrive.

Dumbing Down Regular New York City Public Schools

How many parents throughout the country pick a particular neighborhood to live in because its designated public school is excellent? This is true whether we're talking about people paying more for rent or ownership in affluent pockets in New York such as Tribeca or saving up for a house in the burbs. Carranza's assault on better performing New York City schools became apparent in May 2018. He retweeted a story about *"Wealthy white Manhattan parents"* who at a public meeting on a diversification program *"angrily rant against plan to bring more black kids to their school"* from RawStory.com. The proposal called for giving students who score below grade level priority access to 25% of seats at each of the district's 18 middle schools. On the Upper West Side's District 3, wrote *New York Post* columnist

Michael Goodwin (5/2/18), the proposal would reserve 10% of seats at middle schools for students whose average score on standardized tests was 1, "well-below proficient." 15% would be set aside for those scoring "2," partially proficient in meeting standards. "3" means proficient, and "4" means excel. Predicts Goodwin: "*Teachers would likely teach to the lowest common denominator.*" That leaves 75% of students "*who would remain trapped in the failing schools*" and successful students pushed out to inferior schools.

In July 2018, resolutions from 2 community councils in Queens and 1 in Brooklyn—3 districts with large Asian populations—condemned Carranza's quota plan. Carranza continued to play the race card, denouncing critics of his District 3 middle-school diversity plan for their "*implicit bias.*" In July, the crazed chancellor blasted 80 high schools for screening students based on test scores and grades, calling it bigoted and that the "*system of screens, the system of selectivity …it's segregating our schools.*" Yet, DOE data show that 63% of kids at these schools are black or Hispanic—close to the 68% that they represent in the public-school population. The problem is a shortage of good schools, which is why affluent whites move out of town or send their kids to private schools.

In August 2018, 11 city high schools including Manhattan Hunter Science HS were set to introduce new admissions policies for 2019 to boost the number of disadvantaged children (such as from poor families, living in shelters or whose parents are incarcerated), joining 5 other high schools that had already implemented the plan, as the DOE pushes to "desegregate" Asian and white schools throughout the city at all grade levels. The total number of city schools participating in the desegregation plan had reached 78.

Park Slope is part of trendy Brooklyn. Carranza plans to uproot the existing admissions policies for Brooklyn's District 15 in which 10 of the 11 middle schools used grades, test scores, and attendance in admissions. While Carranza proposed a quota of 25% of seats for the Upper West Side, for the Brooklyn district that includes top middle school MS 51 that de Blasio's 2 kids attended, he would impose quotas based on income, immigration status and homelessness to fill 52% of seats! In liberal Boston, still half-white, desegregation resulted in a public-school system that's now just 12% white, reports the *Post*. It also cites a study finding that 40% of lower-income families now opt out of their neighborhood elementary schools (8/21/18).

The Gifted & Talented program that places top scorers into more selective schools offers another escape hatch from failing public schools. But Carranza wants everyone stuck in the Titanic school system, no lifeboats for anyone. His criticisms rely on statistical misrepresentations. Speaking to District 4 parents in Queens in February 2019, Carranza complained the program *designates "over 35 percent of your students"* as *"gifted and talented,"*—which is *"far beyond the percentage of gifted and talented that, from a statistical perspective, should be found in the population."* Except he has his numbers wrong. According to the DOE, a little over 9,000 or 28% of 32,664 who took the test qualified for either district or citywide G & T programs in 2018. But of all New York City pupils in the kindergarten through 3rd grade seats, only 2.7% qualified for G & T seats.

Then there's de Blasio's School Renewal Program, announced in November 2013, whose early demise was announced on February 26, 2019. When he first came into office, de Blasio refused to close failing schools as did his predecessor, Michael Bloomberg. Bloomberg *"moved students who had been attending failed schools to more effective ones, and the kids experienced academic gains,"* noted Marcus Winters, associate professor at Boston University. Instead, de Blasio poured $773 million beginning in 2014 into fixing 94 failing schools with an extra hour of instruction, special teacher training, and social services for students. Parents were avoiding these schools even before Renewal began, and enrollment continued to decline.

According to the DOE, fewer than 25% of the schools improved enough to exit after 3 years. The *Post*'s "Education Boondoggle" series had previously exposed the enrollment decline, a surge in per-student spending, failure to meet improvement goals, and the hiring of "leadership coaches" for up to $1,400 a day. Three studies on the program's impact—one by Marcus Winters for the Manhattan Institute, another by Teachers College professor Aaron Pallas, and a 3rd by Rand Corporation—found little or no effect on student performance, reports Winters (*NYP*, 2/28/19). The city had to close 23 of its original 94 schools (14 were closed for non-improvement, and 9 merged with other schools), 21 more "graduated out," and the remaining 50 will get the same form of TLC and funding but lose the "Renewal" brand. As of 2018, enrollment in those 50 schools was 17% lower than in 2014-2015, reports Ray Domanico of the Manhattan Institute, while in the same years enrollment in New York charter schools increased by 34% (29,000 students), with thousands on waiting lists. Carranza did his race-baiting shtick, blaming "privilege" when the city's public schools are 80% minority.

Parents and kids from these schools all over the city were furious. One mother of 2 kids at PS 298 in Brownsville, Brooklyn, said: "*Every year they get these big checks. What are they doing with it?*" A mother in Long Island City, Queens where her child attends PS 111, where less than 8% of kids passed state math tests in 2018, fumed: "*There are fights between kids, there are hoodlums everywhere. My daughter is falling apart.*"

School discipline has been the victim of progressive ideology. According to a recent John Jay College report, suspensions peaked at 63,635 in the 2010-2011 school year, and then fell for 6 straight years, dropping nearly 50%. Black kids had the highest suspension rates followed by Hispanics. For progressives "disparate impact" is a sign of bias, and de Blasio alludes to "*the discriminatory use of suspension.*" A Queens high-school teacher told the *Post* on March 7th, "*If I had a dime for every time I was told to suck something, I'd be a millionaire.*" "*I've heard complaints from teachers who don't feel safe,*" reported the state Senate Education Committee chair John Liu (D-Queens).

Here's an example of a teacher not feeling safe because she wasn't. Aida Sehic, a refugee from ethnic cleansing in Bosnia in the early 1990s, now a New York City teacher, filed a federal lawsuit in September 2018 against the DOE, alleging students in Manhattan and the Bronx cracked her nose, stabbed her with a mechanical pencil, trashed her classroom, sexually harassed her, and called her "white bitch" with impunity. Administrators retaliated for reporting these incidents with disciplinary charges in 2016. "*You can't kick the kids out and the administration blames you,*" she told the *Post*. According to her attorney, in March Sehic settled the case with the DOE for a "substantial" sum.

"*Our current discipline system is broken,*" UFT President Michael Mulgrew told the *Post*. City Hall's authority to run the school expires on June 30th if not reapproved by the state legislature. De Blasio defended his "restorative justice" policy adopted during the Bloomberg administration that opts for "counseling" rather than discipline. When students disrupt classes, no one learns, including the black and Hispanic students who form the majority in public schools.

The City College of New York was once the poor man's Harvard. It offered high academic standards and free tuition. In the late 60s, it introduced "open" admissions. Twenty years ago, standards were raised again. More recently, the school under the "progressive" de Blasio administration is backsliding. The City University of New York (CUNY), which includes CCNY, Brooklyn College, and Queens College, dropped the freshman requirement to have passed high school trigonometry or take remedial classes. 62% required remedial classes in 2017, 80% in 2016, while 73% needed remedial math in 2016, only 52% in 2017—because of lowered standards.

<u>False Charges Against Charters</u>

In New York City, charter schools enroll 123,000 city students, a tenth of public-school kids, in 236 schools. Some 53,000 families are on a waiting list. The 2018 lottery for admission to charters attracted nearly 80,000 applicants for just 26,900 seats. The demand for these seats has risen 9% from 2017. Like de Blasio, Carranza attacks charter schools that outperform the public schools held in a death grip by the teachers' union. Despite the fact that 95% of the students in high-ranking Eva Moskowitz's Success Academy network are black and Hispanic, "*De Blasio hates Moskowitz and tries to strangle charters because he is in the pocket of the teachers' unions*," writes Michael Goodwin.

The failure of public schools K-8 to educate black and Hispanic children is the failure of political elites beholden to the UFT. A 2017 report from the IBO tracked 71,000 students from 2008. It found that black and Hispanic kids started 3rd grade behind in math and reading comprehension, with the gap growing by 8th grade. Goodwin notes similar results released in fall 2018 from New York State tests: black and Latino students combined averaged 35% in English proficiency and 28% in math in grades 3-8, while Asians and whites combined averaged 67% in English and in math. Carranza and de Blasio blame the gap on racism, a means of dodging an overhaul of failing public schools.

In 2018, only 6% of black and 8% of Hispanic 7th-graders scored above grade level in math on the annual state assessment tests, compared to 37% for whites and 46% for Asians, reports Stanley Ng, member of the Citywide Council on High Schools.

On the state math exam, 15 of the top 25 high-scoring schools in the city are charters, reports the *Post*, while charters out-performed the regular public schools in English, too.

Eva Moscowitz's **Success Academies**, which operates 47 schools with 17,000 students, posted much higher scores for those state exams. New York City's students averaged 46.7% proficiency in English and 42.7% in math. Success students—93% are nonwhite-- scored 91% in English and 98% in math.

According to a Manhattan Institute analysis of 2018 state exams in grades 3-8, 57% of black city charter kids scored proficient or better in English, but only 30.6% of black students statewide. For Hispanics, charter kids bested statewide, 54.5% v. 22.8%. The gap in math was 25% for both groups. Charters aren't "cream-skimming" the best students, according to a 2018 Temple University study by Sarah Cordes (published in Education Next), which found "*no significant changes in school demographics at district schools after charters' entry that might explain improved student performance.*" Charters admit students by lottery. In 2018 60,000 black kids (52% v. 22.5% at district schools) and 43,000 Hispanic kids (38% v. 41% at district schools) were enrolled in charter schools. Charters today enroll 20,847 students with learning disabilities --18.5% of enrollment as compared to 19.4% in the regular public-school system. 81% of charter kids are "economically disadvantaged," but only 74% in regular public schools (*NYP*, 3/18/19).

The hypocritical anti-screening chancellor was San Francisco's school superintendent when he sent his daughter to the selective and elite Lowell School, a public high school which under court orders had different entrance test cutoffs for different racial and ethnic groups. Now Carranza calls screening "*racially biased.*" Carranza falsely claims charters take resources from other school kids. In February 2019 he whined that state law requires the city pay charters' rent when it denies them space in public-school buildings, but that space is unused space. Charters get less public money per student than regular public schools. Deputy Chancellor Karin Goldmark said rent payments cost the city $100 million, which "*comes out of the New York City school system*" although the city can provide the space at no cost: there are more than 100,000 empty seats in public-school buildings. Writes the director of education policy at the Manhattan Institute, Ray Domanico (*NYP*, 2/19/19): since 2007, charter enrollment in the city has grown by 107,000 while at the same time the DOE's budget for its own schools (after removing the amount that goes to charters) has grown by $7.5 billion despite a 13,000 decrease in enrollment. The UFT always says it needs more money, yet, New York State spent $22,366 per pupil in 2016, 90% above the national average, according to the US Census Bureau, and the city now spends over $24 billion on schools, about $24,000 per pupil.

The real issue is not diverting resources but the UFT's embarrassment at the success of its competition. The Democratic-controlled state legislature in March resisted lifting the cap on charter schools set in 1999 (a statewide cap on the total number and a lower cap on the number permitted in the city). On March 4th, the Haven Charter High School that would offer a "STEM" education in science and technology was approved by the SUNY Board of Trustees. Only 7 slots were remaining but 13 schools had won approval. 6 of the approved charters including Haven (in the Bronx) "*will remain in limbo*" until the cap is removed or the 99 charters still available elsewhere in the state are made available in the city, observed Daniel Diaz, director of East Side House Settlement (*NYP*, 3/6/19). Opponents to lifting the cap are some of the same lefties that drove out Amazon. In 2018 6 pro-charter state senators were unseated by pro-UFT charter critics in primaries. Said State Senator Diane Savino (D-SI): "*All the new members are openly hostile to charter schools.*"

In early February 2019 de Blasio praised a 1.6% rise in city graduation rates. Nearly 76% of public high school students graduated in 2018. That came as a result of lowered passing grades. Test scores in math and ELA Regents exams are down. One reader to the *Post* described the State Education Department as "*a diploma mill printing worthless paper*" (2/6/19). While the deal with Amazon was still on, Mayor de Blasio claimed that many of the promised 25,000 prospective jobs would go to CUNY students and public-housing residents, unlikely because de Blasio and Carranza "*have rejected academic merit as a key standard at the Department of Education,*" *City Journal*'s Bob McManus observed. Instead of preparing kids for the high-tech future, the quota backers are "*embracing homogenized ethnicity as the lodestar of Gotham's public-school system"* that *"explicitly rejects achievement in favor of Carranza's notion of ethnic balance."*

If the city had a functional subway system and competent public-school system it would find it easier to attract Silicon Valley corporations. Newark (and New Jersey) offered Amazon much larger tax breaks than did New York City -- $7 billion. What New York offers is highly skilled workers in the financial and cultural capital of the US. With stifling anti-corporate regulations and demands, however, the city repels prospective businesses. Now it wants to decapitate the few remaining esteemed schools to calm the beast of "social justice." You get what you vote for.

5 GIMME VICTIMHOOD

Elizabeth Warren is a liar. She denies she claimed she was of Indian heritage in order to advance her career. She cannot put this issue to rest. The *Boston Globe* glossed over her academic climb, insisting her rise from downscale Rutgers University to Harvard professor was due to merit. Warren blames the president for making her a laughing stock. She did it to herself. Had she admitted she believed the family lore of Indian ancestry and used that belief to bolster her credentials, she might have been forgiven. Instead, she kept pointing to family tales, high cheekbones, and in near-political suicide, to a DNA test that shows she is as much Native American as your or I. Then came the apologies to Indian tribes she was not a part of, nor ever would be by taking a DNA test. In her announcement of her candidacy in the 2020 presidential race, in Lawrence, Mass., the power-hungry liar did not address the devastation in sanctuary city Lawrence due to the influx of drug-related crime and economic hardship.

In early February, 2019 the *Washington Post* uncovered her 1986 Texas State Bar registration card where she listed her race as "American Indian." Back in 2012, when news first hit that Warren had been recorded as Indian in faculty directories, she said she was unaware of the listing and hadn't asked for it. DNA testing said she might be 1/1024th Native. Warren is now rejected by the right for her advocacy of confiscatory taxes, and by the left for cultural appropriation.

"Believe the woman" was the directive from the #Me Too crowd toward Christine Blasey Ford who alleged an unsubstantiated story of sexual misconduct by Judge Brett Kavanaugh's in his Supreme Court confirmation hearing. "Believe the woman" was not heard coming out of the mouths of most Democrats in the case of Virginia lieutenant governor, **Justin Fairfax**, not only because he's black and a Democrat but because his resignation along with that of Governor Ralph Latham and Attorney General Mark Herring for wearing blackface would leapfrog the next-in-line Republican into the governor's mansion. DNC Chairman Tom Perez called on Northam to resign, which he refused to do. A Quinnipiac Poll, notes Holman Jenkins, Jr. in the *Wall Street Journal* (2/23-24/19), found that 56% of black Virginia voters don't believe the governor should resign over a blackface episode.

On February 24th, Fairfax shocked the Virginia state senate when he donned the mantel of victimhood, comparing calls for his resignation to a lynching: "*I've heard much about anti-lynching on the floor of this very Senate,*" he said, referring to Virginia's General Assembly passing legislation regretting episodes of lynching between 1877 and 1950. "*And yet we stand here in a rush to judgment,*" he went on to say, "*with nothing but accusations and no facts...*"

The Smollett Saga

Victimhood can bestow tangible benefits as it did for Elizabeth Warren. Victimhood can also bestow more subjective goodies such as sympathy, publicity, attention, and maybe even extend your time on a TV show. "Believe the black gay male" was the immediate reaction by the media, celebrities and Democrats to a TV actor's account of a "hate crime."

On January 29th, when news of the attack on Jussie Smollett became public, Senator **Kamala Harris** (D-CA), a former prosecutor who should have known better than to jump the gun, insisted it was a bias attack: "*This was an attempted modern day lynching. No one should have to fear for their life because of their sexuality or color of their skin. We must confront this hate.*" Senator **Cory Booker** (D-NJ) also called the attack "*an attempted modern-day lynching.*" Speaker **Nancy Pelosi** said on January 30th: "*The racist, homophobic attack on @JussieSmollett is an affront to our humanity ... May we all commit to ending this hate once and for all.*" **Al Sharpton** called the attack a "*reminder of the times we live in,*" but backed off from further proclamations. Know-it-all newcomer **AOC** tweeted: "*There is no such thing a 'racially charged'* [reported by "Entertainment Tonight"] *...It was a racist and homophobic attack...It is not one's job to water down or sugar-coat the rise of hate crimes.*" Director **Rob Reiner**, a trumpeter of Trump conspiracy theories (he tweeted well before the Mueller report was completed, *"More digging will have to be done. But there'll be crimes. And we better get to see them."*), weighed in directly with a link to Trump: *"Homophobia existed before Trump, but there is no question that since he has injected his hatred into the American bloodstream, we are less decent, less human & less loving. No intolerance! No DT!"* Ironic--a quest for tolerance juxtaposed with no tolerance of Trump. Not to mention the falsehood of Trump being anti-gay. Maybe Reiner mixed Trump up with Mike Pence. All these remarks quickly disappeared during the next few days as Smollett's credibility came under fire. The false narrative fit perfectly with liberal beliefs that Trump couldn't win without gaming the system, and that hate crimes are precipitated by his rhetoric and policies.

The initial cries of "hate crime" that characterized Smollett's report of a late-night Chicago assault in freezing weather got drowned out in the whirlwind of more details. Smollett claimed he was walking home from a Subway restaurant at 2AM on January 29th when two white men shouting racial slurs— *"Empire faggot nigger"*—and *"This is MAGA country!"* beat him up, threw a noose around his neck, doused him with a chemical, likely bleach. The incident reported by Smollett occurred one week after the Cinespace studio in Chicago received a hate letter directed at the actor— *"You will die black fag"* read the message created by letters cut from a magazine-- with "MAGA" in red letters scribbled on the envelope, and white powder inside (later said to be acetaminophen). There was a photo of a stick figure hanging from a tree with a gun pointed at it. This was shortly before I published *Hate Crimes: Who's to Blame?* I decided not to add the incident in a last-minute addendum. Smollett's account on TV did not ring authentic or sound credible.

Discrepancies in Smollett's account made the news. Initially, Smollett didn't tell the cops about the "MAGA country" soundbite. He didn't use his cellphone to call the cops. He kept the rope around his neck for 40 minutes. The brothers arrested for the crime didn't fit the profile of attackers given by Smollett. Olabinjo and Abimbola Osundairo, who both worked on "Empire," told cops they were hired by Smollett as the "attackers." Chicago Police Superintendent Eddie Johnson told "Good Morning America" host Robin Roberts that the brothers became cooperating witnesses in the 47th hour of the 48 hours cops were allowed to hold them. To fake the attack, the brother bought ski masks, a red hat, and a rope, caught on videotape, with the $100 Smollett gave them. They selected a spot near Smollett's apartment because the actor believed a surveillance camera would record the staged attack. Smollett called police attention to the camera, which cops found strange because it faced the wrong way. Sources said Smollett was upset that the letter didn't get a "bigger reaction." A review of some 50 surveillance cameras, some hidden in residential doorbells, including in the Streeterville neighborhood where Smollett lives, helped police establish the brothers' movements. Smollett, 36, paid the brothers $3,500 upfront to stage the assault. Then came suspicions that Smollett himself wrote the letter. He did not return for another interview with Chicago cops. He refused to relinquish his phone.

The brothers were released on February 18th and issued a statement to CBS: "*We are not racist. We are not homophobic, and we are not anti-Trump. We were born and raised in Chicago and are American citizens.*" The FBI took over the case and a grand jury delivered an indictment on charges of filing a false police report. The big news on February 21st was Smollett's arrest on felony disorderly conduct charges for allegedly filing a false police report. Investigators substantiated the brothers' claim that Smollett played a role in the letter delivered to Cinespace studio on January 22nd. Scenes featuring Smollett on the TV show "Empire" have been edited, with 5 of 9 scenes and a musical number excised, TMZ reported. The show scrubbed his character, Jamal Lyon, from the last 2 episodes of the season.

To his credit, race-baiter Al Sharpton, who decades ago gave us the bogus attack on Tawana Brawley claiming to have been raped by four white men, now said on his show, "Politics Nation" on MSNBC, that if Smollett and the body-building brothers staged the attack, "*they ought to face accountability to the maximum*". New York City Council Speaker Corey Johnson apologized for initially calling the incident "*an attempted modern-day lynching.*"

Superintendent Johnson announced that Smollett "*took advantage of the pain and anger or racism to promote his career.*" The black superintendent was left asking, "Why?" The answer was Smollett wanted to boost his career and his salary, reported as $100,000 per episode. "*Most shameful of all,*" declared the *Post* (2/22/19), when Smollett learned cops had made 2 arrests, he was set to make an official complaint until he learned it was Ola and Abel Osundairo. Smollett was friends with Abel who reportedly supplied him with ecstasy. In

2007, Smollett pleaded no contest to providing false information to LA cops during a traffic stop for drunk driving, identifying himself as his brother. Smollett says he's being railroaded by the "system." His lawyer denies the "*outrageous allegations.*" Smollett was freed on $100,000 bail.

In March, Smollett was indicted on 16 felony counts that includes 2 allegedly false statements to 2 different police officers. He pleaded not guilty. Smollett faced up to 3 years in prison if convicted. The most horrific part of this charade was the noose. Supt. Johnson asked: "*Why, would anyone, especially an African-American man, use the symbolism of a noose to make false accusations?*" Out of the blue, on March 26, 2019, Cook County prosecutors dismissed the case while saying this was not an exoneration but "*just punishment*"—18 hours of community service at Jesse Jackson's PUSH Coalition and forfeiture of his $10,000 bond--and sealed Smollett's record. Chicago police were livid. Mayor Rahm Emanuel called him a "liar." What the mayor called a "*whitewash of justice*" involved cushy comforts at the precince: no handcuffs, no jail cell. President Trump called the case "*an absolute embarrassment to our country.*" On March 28th, Chicago officials gave Smollett one week to cough up $130,106.15 to defray the cost of the probe. Smollett's legal team, proclaiming Jussie's innocence, said it was Chicago's mayor and police chief who owed Smollett "*an apology.*" One of his lawyers claimed that the 2 black brothers attacked Smollett wearing "*whiteface.*"

Michelle Obama's former chief of staff Tina Tchen had contacted prosecutor Kim Foxx earlier and put her in touch with a Smollett family member. Foxx unsuccessfully tried to get the FBI to take over the case at that family member's request. Her so-called recusal from the case on February 13th did not entail recusal of her office. Following dismissal of the case, the police union got the FBI to review this peculiar denouement. Foxx was said to be a social justice prosecutor to whom, according to *Breitbart*'s Joel Pollak, billionaire far-left activist George Soros donated $408,000 to super PACS supporting Foxx's primary and general campaign for Cook County state's attorney. Michelle Malkin disclosed Tchen's other Obama connections: the "*deep-pocketed campaign finance mega-bundler*" who also served as Obama's special assistant "*shoveled more than $200,000 into the 2008 Obama campaign coffers.*" Justice for the well-connected.

Faux Hate Crimes

Belatedly, some in the media noted the message of hate directed at Trump supporters. The president himself tweeted when disclosures turned his sympathy sour: *"@JussieSmollett—what about MAGA and the tens of millions of people you insulted with your racist and dangerous comments!? #MAGA."* DNC Chairman Tom Perez spoke of a "surge" in hate crimes when asked about Smollett's fraudulent claim on "Fox News Sunday" (2/24/19). In *Hate Crimes: Who's to Blame?* — published soon after the Smollett saga began—I discuss some of the difficulties in assessing the 17% hate crime increase in 2017 in the US, led by anti-Semitic crimes, reported by the FBI. One problem is the difficulty in distinguishing between increased reporting and an increased number of incidents. Numerous bogus incidents have been reported in which the fake victim initially blames racists, which the press duly notes. Later come the retractions. There are political assumptions made that cannot be verified—some later contradicted by the evidence--that the attacks are by white supremacists. The Anti-Defamation League reports that rightwing extremist violence accounts for about 73% of terrorist murders in the US in the past decade (Eli Lake, *NYP*, 3/22/19), but ADL statistics have been controversial. White supremacist massacres—whether at the Pittsburgh synagogue or New Zealand church—so traumatic to all of us-- should not obscure the numerous leftist attacks against conservatives and attacks by pro-Palestinian groups against Jewish students on college campuses that are not counted as hate crimes.

In addressing his article on how the media perpetuate the notion that Trump's election (and the Brexit vote) have increased hate crimes ("Snowplow Politics, *NR*, 1/28/19), Douglas Murray notes the element of "bias" that turns a "crime" into a "hate crime," and encouragement by law enforcement to report crimes as hate crimes, *"the better to meet their targets."* Murray concludes, as have others including myself, that *"there are strong reasons to treat the statistics in this particular area with special caution"* (*NR*, 2/25/19).

In the *Wall Street Journal* (2/23-24/19), Holman W. Jenkins, Jr. sees that the *"nature of the racial hoax seems to have changed"* from Tawana Brawley's time, when she was avoiding punishment from her stepfather for an absence from home. *"Recent cases involved mainly perpetrators who wanted to bring attention to themselves, pose as victims, and incite ideological hatred,"* writes Jenkins, who finds that hate-crime laws *"seem to have spawned an epidemic of false charges."* The College Fix, a student-reported news site, list 50 such incidents on campus since 2012. Andy Ngo of *NR* tweeted details of 31 cases involving anti-Trump animus.

Following the Smollett faux attack, Heather Mac Donald, an expert on crime statistics, noted in a *City Journal* column (adapted by the *Post*, 2/22/19) that the 2017 total of 7,000 hate crimes—1,000 more than in 2016—comes with an additional 1,000 police agencies participating in reporting, and that the number in our large country is still *"infinitesimal."* She points out that *"very little black-on-white street crime gets classified"* as hate crimes (although *"Between 2012 and 2015, blacks committed more than 85 percent of interracial violent victimizations between blacks and whites."*) The Smollett case is *"just the latest example of how desperate media elites want to confirm their favored narrative about America: that the country is endemically and lethally racist, sexist and homophobic, and that the election of Donald Trump both proves and reinforces such bigotry."* Mac Donald calls the Smollett case a "rerun" of the Covington hoax (the young man who was smeared by many liberals is now suing the *Washington Post* for defamation) and finds that white elites would rather blame themselves and "deplorables" for *"nonexistent racism"* than speak about the *"academic-skills gap"* that leads to *"socioeconomic disparities."*

The pursuit in New York City of "social justice" for a few minority students in lieu of bridging the academic achievement gap between blacks and Hispanics and white and Asians, leads to dumbing down schools of excellence and abandoning both poor, high-achieving Asian-American students and a majority of black and Hispanic students who fail to thrive. The social justice warriors should be charged with hate crimes and academic malpractice.

In the hearts of progressives, victimhood never ends, not even after death. Speaking on "The Breakfast Club" radio show in February, Senator Kamala Harris (D-CA) proposed reparations for the descendants of black slaves to address *"200 years of slavery."* Not to be outdone, Senator Elizabeth Warren (D-MA), added Native American descendants to the reparations list. Democratic presidential contender, Julian Castro, jumped on board. The argument that slavery's legacy *"explains the current wealth gap between blacks and whites,"* reasons Robert Woodson at *The Hill*, omits the fact that both blacks and Native Americans *"were complicit in the slave trade"* and ignores the achievements of blacks *"throughout history."* In the past both President Obama and Bernie Sanders have ruled out seeking reparations. The notion that the candidate who offers the most freebies will gain the White House seems to be the overriding strategy of these pandering opportunists.

6 GIMME WHITEWASH

"We can't have one standard for Steve King and another for Northam"—former Rep. Donna Edwards

The #Me Too crowd that wanted Republicans to "believe the woman" and accept on faith Christine Blasey Ford's belated and unproven allegations against Judge Brett Kavanaugh hid when more serious and better substantiated allegations of sexual assault were leveled against Virginia's Lt. Governor **Justin Fairfax**. Fairfax rejected claims by Vanessa Tyson, a California political science professor, that he forced her to perform oral sex in 2004 during the Democratic National Convention in Boston. *"By December 2017, I not only told many friends that Mr. Fairfax had sexually assaulted me but I also reached out to a personal friend at The Washington Post and spoke to his colleague about the assault,"* she wrote. He refused to resign even after Meredith Watson, came forward to say he'd raped her in 2000 when they were both Duke Students. DNC Chairman Tom Perez calls for an "independent investigation" into the claims by the two women of Fairfax's sexual misconduct. Fairfax refuses to cooperate with a public hearing that Republicans have suggested.

The reason that the Democratic Party would not take the high ground in the Fairfax case to refute claims of hypocrisy was the perilous position of its two leading white politicians. Governor **Ralph Northam**'s medical school 1984 yearbook page showed two young men, one in blackface, one wearing a KKK hood. The governor apologized, admitted to wearing blackface, and then retracted the confession, saying neither photo was of him, while explaining he'd once worn blackface at a dance contest to mimic Michael Jackson. He claimed during an interview with CBS anchor Gayle King that he first saw the photo when a conservative website, Big League Politics, displayed it on February 1st. Suffering foot-in-mouth disease, Northam referred to slaves as "*indentured servants.*" He refused to resign, claiming that as a doctor he was uniquely qualified to heal his state whose history was rife with racism. No one thought Virginia was sick—just its leaders. His predicament was poetic justice for smearing Republican Ed Gillespie as racist in the 2017 gubernatorial race. Third on the governing totem pole was AG Mark Herring, who confessed to having donned blackface in high school.

Were all 3 leaders to simultaneously resign, the next governor would be a Republican (Speaker of the House of Delegates, Kirk Cox). Can't have that. While offensive racial postures were equated with racism, a majority of black Virginians forgave the governor, and many gave both red-faced politicians a pass on blackface: they were young, they're contrite, and they're Democrats. DNC Chair Tom Perez called for Northam to resign but not Fairfax. Some folks judged the blackface episodes as heinous as the alleged criminal sexual assaults committed by Fairfax. Some compared the allegations against Fairfax—he admitted to a consensual relationship with both accusers—to those against Brett Kavanaugh although Christine Blasey Ford could not substantiate her claim that Kavanaugh even attended the party where the assault allegedly occurred. With some exceptions, Democrats suddenly recalled the quaint Republican notion of due process.

Blackface is an anachronism. It existed in minstrel shows from the 1830s onward and in film, such as in the late 1920s by jazz singer Al Jolson. Many whites found it entertaining, and even today many people view it as racially insensitive but not indicative of racism; blacks found it demeaning. Host Megyn Kelly got the ax from NBC for talking about blackface as a non-controversial entertainment several decades ago. The network construed this as approval and with her ratings in the tank she had to go. *Washington Examiner* writer Eddie Scarry named entertainers who've dabbled in blackface: late- night comic, **Jimmy Kimmel**, who in a skit for "The Man Show" mocked NBA player Karl Malone, NBC's **Jimmy Fallon**, who appeared in a SNL skit portraying Chris Rock, **Billy Crystal**, who used to impersonate Sammy Davis, Jr., and **Ted Danson**, who dressed in minstrel attire at a 1993 roast of Whoopi Goldberg. Fox News' "Watters World" (2/9/19) mentioned another celebrity who once wore blackface--**Robert Downey Jr**. in a piece that rebuked the *New York Times* for manipulating the meaning of racism—a feeling of superiority—to paint scenes in *Mary Poppins* as "racist" in which the characters (played by Julie Andrews and Dick Van Dyke) are smudged with soot.

Lawmakers are so fearful of offending racial and ethnic groups that have suffered discrimination that they try to legislate tolerance. New York City's Human Rights Commission issued new guidelines on February 18th prohibiting discrimination based on a person's hairstyle. The guidelines focused in particular on black dos. *"There is a widespread and fundamentally racist belief that black hairstyles are not suited for formal settings, and may be unhygienic, messy, disruptive, or unkempt,"* proclaimed the commission, which said such beliefs *"are often rooted in white standards of appearance and perpetuate racist stereotypes that black hairstyles are unprofessional."* I'm not sure what a "disruptive" hairdo means, but I'm guessing the Marine buzzcut won't soon be replaced by dreadlocks.

Cowardly college administrators routinely cave to student activists demanding political purity. The Association of Black Harvard Women and other groups called for removal of Ronald Sullivan as faculty dean of Winthrop House, a dorm, because he joined the legal defense team for sexual predator Harvey Weinstein. The leader of the student petition against Sullivan, the *Post* reports, is Danukshi Mudannayake, who calls his work for the movie mogul *"deeply trauma-inducing."* Harvard's dean of freshman is launching a *"climate review"* of Sullivan.

During a speech at the Conservative Political Action Conference (CPAC), President Trump introduced Hayden Williams, a conservative student punched at Berkeley. Trump signed an executive order requiring colleges support free speech if they want federal research dollars. Well-endowed universities could withstand that reprisal, writes Karol Markowicz, who mentions Heterodox Academy, formed by professors, administrators, and grad students to promote viewpoint diversity on campus (*NYP*, 3/11/19). In December 2018, the DOJ got the University of California to agree to protect controversial speakers. Betsey McCaughey reports that First Amendment advocates are suing the University of Texas for using "bias squads" to punish students for offensive comments, and FIRE (Foundation for Individual Rights in Education) reports that over 90% of colleges restrict speech through speech codes, "bias squads" and the hecklers' veto.

In March the House passed a voting rights bill (234-193) not likely to be taken up in the Republican-controlled Senate that would restore voting rights to convicted felons and require super-PACS that spend money in campaigns to disclose names of donors giving more than $10,000. Another attempt by the Democratic Party to control speech, Pelosi's HR-1— "For the People Act"—tellingly opposed by the ACLU-- would regulate any speech that "*promotes or supports the candidate, or attacks or opposes the candidate,*" thereby restricting the speech of unions, business groups, and advocacy groups.

Some regulations to protect the small but vocal transgender community endanger a larger community. A recent New York law gives biological males who now identify as women access to women's bathrooms, locker rooms, and even battered women's shelters. Feminist organizations are not making waves about the new law or other transgender issues that affect women and girls, observes Abigail Shrier of *City Journal.* She asks whether girls have "*no reason to feel threatened confined within the tiled walls of a locker room with a person possessing full male genitalia—as 89 percent of trans women do?*" Or take the situation of female athletes "*being unfairly bested by boys whose muscle mass and bone density confer an unearned advantage.*" Schrier notes that "*The fox has entered the henhouse,*" but "*women's organizations stick to the fiction that both species are hens.*"

Just as liberals are now being consigned to the dung-heap by socialist progressives, so early-day feminists are maintaining their silence in the face of social and sports initiatives that harm women but placate the transgender community. One opponent of transgender nuttiness is gay icon and pioneer for gay athletes, **Martina Navratilova**, the star tennis player who came out in 1981, a supporter of the 1st transgender woman pro-tennis player, Renee Richards. Navratilova doesn't suffer fools or foolishness. Her response when asked by a reporter whether she was still gay, legend has it, was, "*Are you still the alternative?*". In December 2018, she protested transgender women--with male genitalia--competing against biological women in sports. In an editorial entitled, "Martina's Still a Standout" (2/21/19), the *Post* defends the tennis star "*now being demonized by gay groups for publicly stating an obvious truth:*

Transgender women athletes have 'unfair physical advantages.'" She called it *"cheating"* in the *Sunday Times* of London. She distinguishes those who've had reassignment surgery from those who merely identify as female and take hormones that do not level the playing field when it comes to the sex differences in muscle mass, including heart muscle, bone density, and lung capacity and oxygen saturation. In response, a nonprofit called "Athlete Ally" that battles homophobia in sports gave her the boot from its board and as its ambassador. I can't figure out what homophobia has to do with gender dysphoria or gender reassignment.

At Connecticut state track championships two biological male transgender runners won the 55-meter dash. Their advantage—testosterone- - predates birth. The testosterone surge in puberty drives athletic advantages—height, speed, muscularity, greater oxygen capacity, writes David Epstein (*WSJ*, 3/16-3/17/19), so that by 14, the fastest high-school boys are beating women's world records. Transgendered long-distance runner Joanna Harper admits that despite testosterone suppression, *"I've been on hormone therapy for 15 years, and I carry more muscle mass than a woman my size, absolutely."*

"There must be some standards," Navratilova says. Are there standards in political debates? In late-night TV monologues? Are there standards for squishy academic disciplines that confuse progressive cant with reasoning, malarkey with scholarship? Navratilova believes sports standards should preclude someone *"having a penis and competing as a woman."* Good luck with that and may your serve always be with you.

We now have numerous tyrannies by minorities within minorities. The once-marginalized have become the powerbrokers. Hard to believe that the transgender community makes up about 0.1%-0.5% of the US population. Roger Kimball wrote about American novelist EJ Levy getting grief for her upcoming historical novel *The Cape Doctor* about James Barry, née Margaret Ann Buckley, a 19th century Irish surgeon who practiced in Cape Town and lived as a man, referred to as "she". Publisher Little, Brown has been bombarded by protests against the *"theft of one of our very few well-documented transgender ancestors,"* as one missive put it. The author dismisses the *"troll mob,"* saying, *"there's no evidence Barry considered herself trans."* As folks slip into subservience when it comes to protecting or advancing members of their own group—be it sexual or ethnic or professional—we might well recall the advice of Hillel: If I'm not for me, who will be for me?

The Constitution's barring of a religious litmus test for government office-holders does not alter today's liberal dogma that religious beliefs mask bigotry. Particularly annoying to liberal legislators are Roman Catholics. They offend liberal sensibilities not only with the official censure of homosexuality but with their objections to abortion on demand, any time, fetus, newborn be damned. Hence, the bragging by New York Governor **Andrew Cuomo**, who on January 22nd signed the extreme abortion-rights bill passed by the Democratic-controlled state legislature that permits 3rd-trimester abortion. Cuomo thumbed his progressive nose at the Catholic Church by having One World Trade Center lighted pink. The new law, in Orwellian fashion called the Reproductive Health Act, moves abortion from the penal code to public health law. That law downgraded the recent murder of a pregnant mother and her baby to a single count of homicide. After Anthony Hobson allegedly stabbed to death Jennifer Irigoyen, who was in her 2nd trimester, Queens DA Richard Brown announced that Hobson would be charged with 2nd-degree murder and 2nd-degree abortion, but had to drop the abortion charge.

The law is far from mainstream. According to a recent Gallup poll, only 13% support 3rd-trimester abortion. According to the Guttmacher Institute, some 12,000 late-term abortions take place annually in the US (1.3% of abortions take place after the 20th week, so, with 926,200 abortions annually, that comes to 12,000 that occur after week 20), but "*Almost none out of medical necessity*," writes former New York Lt. Gov. Betsey McCaughey (*NYP*, 2/14/19). That is more than the number of gun homicides reported by the FBI, Ramesh Ponnuru points out (*NR*, 2/25/19). Most are not due to fetal abnormalities which, according to researcher Diana Greene Foster (University of California, San Francisco) "*make up a small minority of later abortions*," and even fewer due to threats to the mother's health. A Guttmacher review of the literature in 2013, Ponnuru writes, concluded that most post-20-week abortions are not performed "*for reasons of fetal anomaly or life endangerment.*"

Especially ghoulish is the provision in the new law to permit withholding treatment of newborns who survive chemically-induced abortions (10% of late abortions are induced with drugs). "*Even if you are pro-choice, as I am,*" writes McCaughey, "*this grisly denial of the value of the nearly born and newly born shocks the conscience.*" This extreme makeover of morality is part of Democratic policy. Senator Patty Murray (D-WA) in February blocked a Senate bill that required doctors to treat abortion survivors, and Senator Kirsten Gillibrand (D-NY), the consummate opportunist now running for president, has called any restrictions of abortion "*an attack on women's rights.*"

While, as Ponnuru points out, neither the Supreme Court nor New York law requires fetal anomaly or life endangerment for a late abortion to be legal, politicians still dance around the issue even as they endorse ever more extreme legislation. **Ralph Northam**, the embattled governor of Virginia, supports a Virginia bill that Kathy Tran, a member of the Virginia House of Delegates, said would allow a pregnant woman at term and in labor to have an abortion. She later ate her words, saying infanticide was illegal in Virginia, while Northam fibbed (again), suggesting very late abortions were done only in cases of severe deformity or when the fetus wasn't viable. His observation that in such cases the infant would be delivered, resuscitated if the family so wished, and "*then a discussion would ensue between physicians and the mother*" ignited an uproar that flabbergasted the former pediatric neurosurgeon.

Current bans on late-term abortion permit it to promote the "health"— i.e., mental well-being—of the mother. In 2007, the USSC upheld the federal ban on partial-birth abortion because other modalities remained legal. With Trump having placed 2 conservative justices on the Court, and with a fragile Ruth Bader Ginsburg at 85, states are enacting ever more extreme abortion laws, just in case *Roe v. Wade* is overturned.

Federal judicial nominee Brian Buescher was subjected to an unseemly grilling in his confirmation hearing by Senators **Kamala Harris** (D-CA) and **Mazie Hirono** (D-HA), who objected to his membership in the world's largest Catholic charitable institution, the Knights of Columbus. On January 16th, the Senate agreed to Nebraska Republican Ben Sasse's resolution "*that disqualifying a nominee to federal office on the basis of membership in the Knights of Columbus violates the Constitution of the United States.*" Liberals, of course, were up in arms when a conservative Fox host questioned the fidelity of a Muslim legislator to the Constitution. Regarding Rep. Ilhan Omar wearing a hijab, former Westchester judge Jeanine Pirro asked on her March 9th show,

"Justice with Judge Jeanine": "*Is her adherence to this Islamic doctrine indicative of her adherence to Sharia law, which in itself is antithetical to the United States Constitution?*" Pirro was off the air the next Saturday, much to the president's chagrin. Omar, who questions the loyalty of American Jews, remains on the Foreign Affairs Committee. In late March, Pirro's suspension ended.

On February 5, 2019, Sen. **Cory Booker** (D-NJ) grilling judicial nominee Neomi Rao, asked, "*Have you ever had an LGBTQ law clerk?*" Her reply: "*I have not been a judge, so I don't have any law clerks.*" Does she now have anyone working for her who is LGBTQ? he persisted. Her reply: "*To be honest, I don't know the sexual orientation of my staff. I take people as they come, irrespective of their race, ethnicity, sexual orientation.*" Booker went on to ask whether gay relationships were a "sin," to which Rao replied, "*Whatever my personal views are on the subject, I would faithfully follow the precedent of the Supreme Court.*" Rao, raised in an immigrant family of Zoroastrian tradition, converted to Judaism when she got married. Booker blew his 2020 presidential candidacy at the starting line.

The culture war on historical accuracy fuels the controversy over monuments of figures no longer held in esteem by progressive viewers—from Christopher Columbus to Robert E. Lee, the ostensible catalyst to the Charlottesville attack, to pioneers in a range of fields who are today considered racist or misogynist. Governor Andrew Cuomo had statues of Confederate war heroes Lee and Stone Wall Jackson removed from a public gallery. Leftist textbooks on American history have been colorized to promote minor figures and demean major ones. Guardians of our culture and history are more discomfited by progressive criticism than angered by the deranged call for censorship of art that depicts American life as it was in bygone eras.

The most recent target of progressive rage by college students are the 12 murals of Christopher Columbus dating to the 19th century at the University of Notre Dame. The school capitulated. The murals will be "shrouded," which its president, the Rev. John Jenkins, says will tell "*the full story*" of Columbus. Observed Roger Kimball, editor of the *New Criterion*, "*Welcome to the new Orwellian world where censorship is free speech and we respect the past by attempting to elide it.*" This is yet another instance in which, Kimball notes, a vocal minority, claiming victim status, demands the destruction, removal or concealment of some object of which they disapprove. These acts of censorship constitute *"an attack on the past for failing to live up to our contemporary standards of virtue."* Kimball quotes Marxist Herbert Marcuse's 1965 essay on "Repressive Tolerance," a "totalitarian classic" in which he promotes *"liberating tolerance,"* that he defined as *"intolerance against movements from the Right, and toleration of movements from the Left."* Sound like Antifa? College kids? MSNBC? Late-night comics?

7 GIMME THAT OLE TIME SCAPEGOAT

In the old days in America, there was anti-Semitism. Nothing like the virulent strain resistant to eradication in Europe. It became particularly prominent in the US in the first half of the 20th century. Had you asked Jewish immigrants from Eastern Europe why they voted Democratic in the late 19th and early 20th centuries, they might have mentioned the social ideals rampant in the Russian Pale of Settlement. Many Jews were drawn to the economic hopes of socialism and Marxism. Once they were settled in America, they might have mentioned the very vocal right-wingers who expressed anti-Jewish sentiments frequently and with fervor. These included nativists in the 1920s bent on restricting immigration to folks from northern Europe.

The political rightwing included prominent trail-blazing automobile manufacturer **Henry Ford**, whose anti-Semitic broadsides were published by his publication, *The Dearborn Independent*, which he purchased in 1918. It ran for 8 years, distributed at every Ford franchise across the country, disseminating conspiracy theories and reprinting the Czarist forgery, *The Protocols of the Elders of Zion*, on purported Jewish conspiracy for world dominion. At President Woodrow Wilson's behest, peacenik Ford switched from Republican to Democrat to run for the senate in 1918 as a supporter of the League of Nations. The League and Ford both lost. Ford's *The International Jew, the World's Foremost Problem* influenced the rise of Nazism. Rebuked for his anti-Semitic campaign by President Wilson and other leading Americans in 1921, and following a 1927 libel suit, Ford closed his newspaper, and in a letter to the Anti-Defamation League renounced views to which he reportedly still clung. Hitler tipped his hat to Ford in *Mein Kampf* and in 1931 told a reporter for the *Detroit News* that Ford was an *"inspiration"* to him. When American merchant ships were torpedoed by German subs in 1939, Ford blamed a conspiracy of financial warmongers, referring to Jews, whom he'd also blamed for World War I.

Then there's the propagator of *Social Justice*. No, I don't mean today's so-called progressives, but the newspaper *Social Justice* of **Father Coughlin**, an enormously popular Canadian-born Roman Catholic priest whose anti-Semitic weekly radio broadcasts reached 30 million in the States in the mid-1930s. He became a thorn in FDR's side, criticizing his monetary and foreign policies. In 1934, he established the National Union for Social Justice, a workers' rights organization that called for nationalizing industry and the railroads. By 1936, Coughlin saw Hitler and Mussolini as a defense against Communism. He subscribed to the Jewish Bolshevism conspiracy of the Russian Revolution. *Social Justice* reprinted *The Protocols of the Elders of Zion* in weekly installments. The last straw for some of his audience was his reaction to Kristallnacht in November 1938. Referring to Christians murdered by Communists in Russia, Coughlin said, *"Jewish persecution only followed after Christians first were persecuted."* In New York City, WINS and WMCA canceled his program. Today liberals bristle when Trump attacks "fake news." But Trump has never shut down a newspaper or suppressed free speech. After the outbreak of World War II in Europe in 1939, the Roosevelt administration forced the cancellation of Coughlin's radio program and prohibited distribution by mail of his newspaper.

And then there was the hero aviator who in 1927 flew nonstop from Long Island to Paris, whose child was kidnapped and murdered in 1931 in the crime of the century, **Charles Lindbergh**. He became spokesman in 1940 of the American First Committee that unsuccessfully tried to steer the US from entering World War II. Despite Hitler's conquests in Europe, Lindbergh opposed the Lend-Lease bill to help out Britain. In a 1941 AFC rally, he named the 3 groups pressing for war: *"the British, the Jewish, and the Roosevelt administration."* Of American Jews, he said: *"Their greatest danger to this country lies in their large ownership and influence in our motion pictures, our press, our radio and our government."*

Sounds like Michigan's freshman Congresswoman Ilhan Omar. FDR said to Treasury Secretary Henry Morgenthau, *"I am absolutely convinced Lindbergh is a Nazi."* He wrote to Secretary of War Henry Stimson: *"When I real Lindbergh's speech, I felt it could not have been better put if it had been written by Goebel himself."* Not surprisingly, Lindbergh communicated with the anti-Semitic, pro-German US Ambassador to England, **Joseph Kennedy**, at the time of the Munich appeasement agreement that Hitler soon violated. Lindbergh was friends with **Henry Ford**, who famously told a former Detroit FBI agent in 1940, *"When Charles comes out here, we only talk about the Jews."* Publicly rebuked by FDR for his views, Lindbergh in 1941 resigned his commission in the Army Air Force. Nevertheless, after Pearl Harbor, Lindbergh flew 50 combat missions in the Pacific as a civilian. While married to Anne Morrow, Lindbergh squirreled away 3 secret families in Germany, fathering 7 kids abroad between 1958 – 1967.

I've written of these early-bird hate specials in several books, as well as the growth and nourishment of anti-Semitism on the Left (see *The Newcomers, The SLJ: Self-Loathing Jews in America*, and just published *Hate Crimes: Who's to Blame?*).

Anti-Semitism in Europe has exploded in recent years. Anti-Israel sentiment is coupled with pro-Palestinian physical assaults on Jews and classical anti-Semitic tropes and vandalism. The BDS movement in both the US and Europe is an exercise in anti-Semitism, ignoring the human rights violations of the most debased dictators in the world, and singling out Israel for social and economic isolation because it protects the Jewish homeland from incursions by uncompromising Palestinians. Britain's Labour Party— headed by the most notorious anti-Semite in the UK, **Jeremy Corbyn**—has been shedding anti-Semitic MPs, but remains an anti-Israel stronghold. In February 2019, 9 members quit the party, citing its problem of anti-Semitism. One of the quitters called the party *"institutionally anti-Semitic."* The party has enrolled younger hard-left members, reports Erielle Davidson at *The Federalist*, causing a gap with more moderate MPS, similar to what's happening in the Democratic Party.

During the "yellow-vest" anti-government protests in France, anti-Semitism again reared its ugly head. Anti-Semitic outbursts have come from groups on the far-right and far-left. Polls show that 44% of yellow-vest protesters believe in the existence of a global Zionist conspiracy, reports Robert Zaretsky at Real Clear World. Riots by anti-Zionists led President Emmanuel Macron to recognize their hatred as a *"reinvented form of anti-Semitism."*

In December, 2018, a Jewish cemetery near Strasbourg, which lies close to the German border, was vandalized. On February 16th, 2019, during the 14th weekend of protests in France—some 5,000 in Paris--yellow-vest protestors were filmed calling academic Alain Finkielkraut *"a dirty Zionist shit."* The ringleader, who was detained on a charge of hate speech, was said to have ties to the Salafi movement in 2014. Interviewed, Finkielkraut spoke of a new type of "anti-racist" anti-Semitism that compares Israeli "colonization" of Palestine with Nazism. A German judge proved his point in March, ruling that 3 Palestinians firebombing a synagogue was not anti-Semitic but a political act, calling *"attention to the Gaza conflict"* (see *Hate Crimes: Who's to Blame?*). Norway's top prosecutor similarly found that a rapper hired by the city of Oslo who ranted against *"fucking Jews"* expressed *"dissatisfaction with the policies of the State of Israel,"* notes the *Federalist's* David Harsanyi.

Dozens of graves in a village near Strasbourg were vandalized—more than 80 graves were defaced with swastikas-- days after yellow-vest protestors were filmed accosting the Jewish academic. Earlier in February, reports the *WSJ*, "Juden" was spray-painted on Bagelstein, a chain of bagels, and a swastika defaced a portrait of Simone Veil, an Auschwitz survivor who became president of the European Parliament and died in 2017. In 2018 police recorded a 74% surge in reported anti-Semitic offenses, notes the *WSJ*. Marches against anti-Semitism were held across France, home to the largest number of Jews in Europe, on February 19th, 2019 (*WSJ*).

Near Brussels, the Aalst Carnival parade *"is known for ruthlessly mocking everyone and everything,"* noted the *New York Times* (3/9/19), *"But critics say it went too far this year."* One float in the March 3rd parade carried *"two giant figures of Orthodox Jews, with side curls and grotesquely large noses, sitting on bags of money. Another group paraded in the white hoods and robes of the Ku Klux Klan."* Said the director of the Brussels branch of the American Jewish Committee, Daniel Schwammenthal, *"It's shocking beyond belief that within living memory of the Holocaust a Carnival parade in Europe would peddle such vile anti-Semitism."* By March 8th, more than 8,000 signed a petition on Change.org calling on

UNESCO to sever ties with the Carnival. The money angle tied to Jews is a classic anti-Semitic trope that Rep. Ilhan Omar aims at both American gentiles and Jews to explain US foreign policy. *"The sight of anti-Semitic caricatures surrounded by money is indistinguishable from imagery used by the Nazis and is grossly offensive in a country where 25,000 Jews were murdered in the Holocaust,"* said Moshe Kantor, president of the European Jewish Congress.

Tolerant Germany tolerates terrorist organizations. Britain in March 2019 banned Hezbollah, the Iranian proxy terrorist group headquartered in Lebanon. It had already banned its military arm in 2008. Germany has refused entreaties by the US, Israel, and some Arab states to do the same, report Mark Dubowitz and Benjamin Weinthal (of the Foundation for Defense of Democracies). The Netherlands is the only EU country that outlawed the entire organization in 2004. Germany, the authors write, is a *"hotbed of Hezbollah activity,"* including fundraising, recruiting, and spreading anti-Semitic ideology. Hezbollah violates Germany's "Basic Law," Interior Minister Horst Seehofer has declared, because it *"fights the right of the existence of the State of Israel with terrorist means,"* yet he, as well as Chancellor Angela Merkel, refuse to clamp down on Hezbollah because, write the authors, of the policy of *"appeasing Iran."*

Blatant anti-Semitism within the GOP has dimmed although it has not been expunged. The blatant anti-Semitism within the Democratic Party is appalling, growing, and ignored by its more grounded members. Even now—despite one of its members failing to disguise her hate. Anti-Israel she obviously is. She leavened her hate speech with classic anti-Semitic tropes to smear all American Jews and Israel's remaining congressional supporters. I first wrote of the freshman Congresswoman from Minnesota, **Ilhan Omar**, in *Hate Crimes* because of her past peddling of anti-Semitic conspiracy theories. She wrote on Twitter that Israel *"has hypnotized the world"*—yup, that tiny country that at birth survived invasion by multiple Arab armies, and is now the object of the BDS movement and the obsession of despots at the UN. She also said, *"May Allah awaken the people and help them see the evil doings of Israel."* Somali-born Omar calls so much attention to herself because, inexplicably, she sits on the House Foreign Affairs Committee, where the anti-Semitic BDS movement now has an ally, one who *"checks each of Natan Sharansky's 3-D boxes: delegitimization, demonization, and double standards,"* observes *NR* (3/11/19).

Omar accused AIPAC (the American Israel Public Affairs Committee) of ensnaring Congressmen for support of Israel— "*It's all about the Benjamins baby.*" On Sunday, February 10th, Omar responded to a journalist's query about why House Minority Leader Kevin McCarthy would defend Israel "*even if it means attacking free speech rights of Americans*" with her tweet about $100 bills. McCarthy wanted congressional action against Omar and Rep. Rashid Talib (D-MI) for their anti-Semitic rhetoric. In response to another query about who Omar "*thinks is paying American politicians to be pro-Israel,*" she tweeted "*AIPAC!*" Classic anti-Semitic stereotypes include worldwide banks being run by Jews, who engage in international conspiracies to control the media and government. Obviously, Omar does not consider being the sole democracy in the Middle East and a reliable US ally a reason to support Israel. A reality check offered by Barbara Boland in *Spectator USA*: in 2018 pro-Israel groups spent $5 million on lobbying. Boland asks about the "'*Benjamins, baby' from horrendous human-rights abusing Gulf states*" that "*dwarf the pro-Israel money in size.*" Saudi Arabia, the UAE, and Qatar have recently spent more than $50 million on lobbying and think-tank donations.

It took a while before Speaker Pelosi and House leaders condemned Omar in a statement signed by Pelosi, Majority Leader Steny Hover, Majority Whip James Clyburn, Democratic Caucus Chair Hakeem Jeffries, and others: "*Anti-Semitism must be called out, confronted and condemned whenever it is encountered, without exception. Congresswoman Omar's use of anti-Semitic tropes and prejudicial accusations about Israel's supporters is deeply offensive. We condemn these remarks and we call upon Congresswoman Omar to immediately apologize for these hurtful comments.*" But Omar was not stripped of her committee seat as was Rep. **Steve King** (R-Iowa) by Rep. Kevin McCarthy for his racist comments on white supremacy. Omar was forced to apologize, which she did on February 11th —a meaningless exercise in insincerity and gracelessness— ending on a "but" note that "*I reaffirm the problematic role of lobbyists in our politics, whether it be AIPAC, the NRA or the fossil fuel industry.*" AIPAC spent about $3.5 million on lobbying in 2018, a small fraction of what many other lobbyists spent, according to the *New York Post* (2/12/19). Basically, Omar said she was sorry anyone was offended: "*Anti-Semitism is real and I am grateful to Jewish allies and colleagues who are educating me on the powerful history of anti-Semitic tropes. My intention is never to offend my constituents or Jewish Americans as a whole. ... I unequivocally apologize.*"

In late March, far-left MoveOn.org called for 2020 Democratic presidential candidates to boycott the AIPAC meeting that traditionally is a bipartisan affair. Immediately, candidates Kamala Harris, Beto O'Rourke, Elizabeth Warren, and Bernie Sanders said they weren't attending. Non-candidates Speaker Nancy Pelosi, Senate Minority Leader Chuck Schumer, and Rep. Hakeem Jeffries from a mixed Jewish and black district in Brooklyn will attend. The president called Dems anti-Israel and *"anti-Jewish"* (Fox News, 3/22/19).

Omar used her position on the **House Foreign Affairs Committee** to deliver an ad hominem attack against Jewish pro-Israel special envoy for Venezuela, **Elliott Abrams**. In a mid-February hearing on the Trump administration's policy toward Venezuela, Omar misrepresented Abrams' testimony in 1982 during the Reagan administration before the Senate Foreign Relations Committee regarding a massacre in El Salvador, in a series of questions that, according to Jose Cardenas, an official in the George W. Bush administration, were apparently cribbed from an article on Al Jazeera's website. She asked whether Abrams still thinks US policy in El Salvador *"was a fabulous achievement."* Abrams replied: *"From the day that President Duarte was elected in a free election to this day, El Salvador has been a democracy. That's a fabulous achievement."* Omar then actually demanded: *"Yes or no, do you think that massacre was a fabulous achievement that happened under our watch?"* *"That is a ridiculous question, and I will not respond to it,"* Abrams replied. No stopping Omar: *"Yes or no?"* Abrams began, *"No—"* when she injected, *"I will take that as a yes."* He shut her down: *"I am sorry, Mr. Chairman, I am not going to respond to that kind of personal attack."*

In 1984, Cardenas recalled, *"millions of Salvadorans defied guerrilla threats to go to the polls to elect Christian Democrat Duarte over a right-wing candidate,"* and in 1986 in Guatemala another Christian Democrat was elected, Vinicio Cerezo. US policy promoted elections and today free elections are the norm in most of Latin America. *"In an irony that obviously escapes Omar, the only holdouts are left-wing authoritarian regimes in Venezuela, Cuba and Nicaragua, where human rights are being systematically violated,"* observes Cardenas (NYP, 2/16/19). Not only is Omar an unrepentant anti-Semite, she's an irrational leftist extremist.

While traveling to the Horn of Africa, this anti-American ingrate wrote from Eritrea, *"Proud to see peace prosper here,"*—Eritrea being, Benny Avni writes, "*ranked just behind North Korea as the world's most oppressive country.*"

Omar was soon back at anti-Semitic rants. At a panel of "Busboys & Poets" in DC, Omar said she has the right to "*talk about the political influence in this country that says it is OK for people for people to push for allegiance to a foreign country.*" No one is pushing any American for allegiance to Israel, which to Omar doesn't mean dual loyalty, the common canard leveled against American Jews, but a "*singular loyalty,*" claiming "*that the Zionist lobby requires lawmakers, Jewish or otherwise, to pledge undivided fidelity to Israel,*" wrote the *City Journal*'s Seth Barron and Judith Miller (*NYP*, 3/5/19). Then, on March 3rd, Omar tweeted, "*I should not be expected to have allegiance/pledge support to a foreign country in order to serve my country in Congress or serve on committee*" as if she'd been asked to. Omar's mocking of her "*Jewish constituency*" concerned with the "*safety and sanctuary for the people of Israel,*" Barron and Miller point out, is "*an attack on American Jewish identity and Jewish influence.*"

Democrats do not challenge Omar's lies about mistreatment of Palestinians. Israel is not just partner in the war against Islamic jihadism, but a democratic country willing to make peace. For decades, Palestinians, goaded by their leaders, have peddled intransigence, wanting all of "Palestine" rather than their own state. 11 Jewish organizations wrote to Speaker Nancy Pelosi to remove Omar from the Foreign Affairs Committee, mentioning her address at a February 23 fundraiser in Tampa hosted by the Islamic Relief USA, whose parent company has been accused of financing terrorist organizations. VP Mike Pence and House Minority Leader Kevin McCarthy have also called for her ouster from the committee but not Dems who are too scared of losing the young, far-left vanguard in the House. The ADL's Jonathan Greenblatt asked for a House resolution rejecting her remarks. AOC tweeted that "*no one seeks this level of reprimand when members make statements about Latinx + other communities*" and later, "*Where's the resolution against Islamophobia?*"

Where, one might ask, do we actually encounter so-called Islamophobia? The US and its Western allies are in a war against Islamist terrorism. That extremism is being funded overtly and covertly by both US allies such as Saudi Arabia and US enemies such as Iran. So-called moderate Islamic groups are often found to be less than critical of the fanatics they supposedly deplore. Regrettably, white supremacists do engage in horrific attacks against blacks, Jews, Muslims, and leftist adversaries. Racist attacks may in fact be increasing, such as the attack on March 15, 2019 by an Australian self-radicalized white supremacist livestreamed on Facebook at 2 New Zealand mosques that killed 50 and wounded 50. However, anti-Semitic acts in the US as well as in Europe far outnumber anti-Muslim hate crimes. Michael Goodwin notes in his piece on "Dems shield mad haters" (*NYP*, 3/6/19) that "*some far-left groups incorporate anti-Semitism into their global conspiracy theories, others couch their criticism of Israel only in political terms,*" but do not hold despotic regimes to the same standard, while the BDS movement and Students for Justice in Palestine peddle on college campuses the "*standard indoctrination*" that "*equates Zionism with colonialism, and Jews with white oppressors.*" The late senator Daniel Patrick Moynihan denounced the UN's Zionism is racism proclamation decades ago (later rescinded). Leftists including the anti-Israel *New York Times* do not demand Palestinians or other Arabs recognize Israel's right to exist. Several years ago, Rep. Jerrold Nadler wrote about the BDS movement's ultimate aim—the destruction of the State of Israel.

The House resolution (before the New Zealand terrorist attack) passed with 23 Republicans voting nay. It condemned all bias including "Islamophobia" and white supremacism, mentioning the Charlottesville riots in August 2017, the 2015 murder of 9 African-Americans in a South Carolina church by a neo-Nazi, and the October 2018 shooting at a Pittsburgh synagogue. Omar's name wasn't mentioned. Noted Speaker Pelosi on the resolution: "*It's not about her. It's about these forms of hatred.*" House Whip Jim Clyburn said Omar's 4 years in a Kenya refugee camp after fleeing violence in Somalia means bigotry is "*more personal*" to her than to the children of Holocaust survivors. Truth to power: Rep. Liz Cheney (R) called the resolution a "*sham put forward by Democrats to avoid condemning one of their own.*"

If you can know a woman by her friends, keep in mind Omar's supporters: **AOC**, who denounces both capitalism and US foreign policy including US intervention in Afghanistan after 9/11, and who Benny Avni describes as Jeremy Corbyn's "BFF," defended Omar's right to "*hate—oops, 'criticize' Israel.*" So did anti-Semitic Palestinian-American Rep. **Rashid Talib**, who has written a column for wacko anti-Semite Louis Farrakhan's newspaper, *Final Call*, and who boosts her "*beautiful Palestine*" but engages in diatribes against Jews and Israel that are also ignored by fellow Democrats although she sits on the Financial Service Committee. Support followed from 2020 Democratic presidential contenders: self-loathing **Bernie Sanders**, phony Indian **Elizabeth Warren**, and **Kamala Harris**. Then there's anti-Semitic Palestinian-American **Linda Sarsour** of the Women's March. Jews comprise only 2% of the US population today, down from 4% in 1950, John Podhoretz notes, so Omar "*is a member of a larger minority group bullying a smaller minority group.*" Rep. **Jan Schakowsky** (D-Ill), although Jewish, is a supporter of the anti-Israel Democratic organization, J Street. No surprise that she told *Politico* she doesn't consider Omar anti-Semitic. Another leftist freshman supporter of Omar is Rep. **Ayana Pressley**, Podhoretz writes, who called for "*equity in our outrage. Islamophobia needs to be included in this.*" Let's not forget that Omar's newest defender is white supremacist and "anti-Zionist" **David Duke**.

The trio—AOC, Omar, and Talib—don't reflect the House victory in 2018 by moderate Democrats who gained some 40 previously Republican seats, writes John Podhoretz (*NYP*, 3/15/19). Omar and Talib are ideologues who replaced other ideologues: Talib got the Detroit seat of leftist John Conyers, and Omar replaced anti-Semite Keith Ellison. AOC won in a primary over moderate Joe Crowley, whom Podhoretz describes as "*astoundingly lazy,*" by 5,000 votes out of only 25,000.

"Islamophobia" is a pretense of widespread discrimination against Muslims to undermine anti-terrorism efforts and pro-Israel sentiment. To his credit, Mayor de Blasio clearly said that "*Suggesting that support for Israel is beholden to a foreign power is absolutely unacceptable.*" Her talk of "*all about the Benjamins,*" he said, "*aligns with*" centuries "*of that kind of negative comment being thrown at the Jewish community.*" To Governor Cuomo's credit, he spoke on WAMC radio of "*some people*" being "*reluctant to vociferously stand up and condemn*" her anti-Semitism because the "*whole political environment is so charged now.*" Shockingly, Dems remained silent when 2 NYU students blamed Chelsea Clinton for inciting the New Zealand mosque attacks by criticizing Omar. The left exploits all hate crimes to silence its critics.

Omar may have gone too far in attacking former President Barack Obama for "*caging of kids*" at the border and for his use of drones in fighting terrorism— "*We don't want anybody to get away with murder because they are polished.*" This freshman representative doesn't represent America; she represents some global universe beholden to Muslims.

Israel supporter, Rep. **Jerry Nadler**, Chairman of the House Judiciary Committee, knocked *"concerted Right-wing tactics aimed at … distracting and dividing those committed to equality and social justice"* after criticizing Omar's rhetoric. Social justice for whom--those that preach the annihilation of Israel? Why not remove these offensive congresswomen from their powerful committees? Jonathan Tobin's answer is that Democrats fear their hard-left base buy into *"bogus intersectional theories that falsely link the struggle for civil rights in the US to the Palestinian war against Israel's right to exist."* Similarly, The *Federalist's* David Harsanyi writes that Pelosi decided to put *"a doltish Jew-hater with radical positions and absolutely no relevant experience"* on the Foreign Affairs Committee *"to appease the growing anti-Israel contingent in her party."* Courage is in short supply in the US Congress. Just ask Senator Charles Schumer.

Omar, who criticizes Israel and the US but praises Eritrea and ignores the suffering of Venezuelans, women in Muslim countries, and Muslims tormented in camps in China, is given a pass by Democratic leaders who put party unity over decency. In the pre-World War II era, anti-Semitism fueled anti-Zionist opposition to Jewish resettlement everywhere, including Palestine. Today, anti-Zionism is the refuge of anti-Semites. The center of anti-Semitism today is the Middle East, where shocking libels are propagated by Iran, Saudi Arabia, and Palestinians. An ADL survey of 100 nations found anti-Semitism *"twice as common among Muslims than among Christians,"* noted Fareed Zakaria in the *Washington Post*, and *"far more prevalent in the Middle East than the Americas"* (see RH Cheval's *Hate Crimes: Who's to Blame?*).

Following 8 years of the Obama administration's anti-Israel policies, there is a glimmer of hope among architects of US Middle East policy. One is President Trump, who moved the US embassy to Israel's capital, Jerusalem. On March 21st Trump called for the US to recognize Israel's sovereignty over the Golan Heights, captured from Syria in the 1967 Six-Day War, which Syria tried to retake in 1973, and Israel annexed in 1981. Senator Lindsey Graham intends to sponsor a bill in Congress to recognize Israel's control of this crest critical to Israel's security, especially in view of the Iranian and Russian presence in Syria. Another bright light has been Ambassador to the UN Nikki Haley, who left her post in October 2018 (in February, President Trump named her successor, current US ambassador to Canada, Kelly Craft). A third may prove to be a new group called Democratic Majority for Israel, which, according to a report in the *Times* by Jonathan Martin, was formed *"to counter the rising skepticism on the left toward the Jewish state,"* by pollster Mark Mellman, *"alarmed by the party's drift from its long-standing alignment with Israel."* The virulence of anti-Semitism on the Left overshadows that of today's American rightwing extremists.

8 GIMME CITIZENSHIP

"Because for all our outward differences, we, in fact, all share the same proud title, the most important office in a democracy: citizen"—President Barack Obama, Farewell Address

The phrase "illegal alien" went the way of the dodo bird. First, leftists wiped out the distinction between legal immigrants and illegal aliens, by referring to *"undocumented immigrants."* Then they upped the ante by talking of the so-called "right" of foreigners to enter the US, the illegality of a travel moratorium (that was eventually upheld by the Supreme Court), the immorality of border barriers, and the "racist" opposition" of those who talk of protecting US sovereignty. By mid-February 2019, during negotiations on border security, Democrats were referring to illegal aliens as *"law-abiding immigrants"* in their demand to cap ICE detention beds. Talk about voting rights for non-citizen residents creeped in, first focused on school boards, such as in lefty San Francisco, and then on driving licenses for illegals. With the Democratic takeover of New York's state senate in the 2018 midterm elections, Democrats controlled all branches of local and state government, and on February 15, 2019 immigrant advocates renewed their push to get driver's licenses for illegals, supported in New York by several officials including Gov. Andrew Cuomo. 12 states and DC already allow illegal immigrants to get licenses. In opposition to Trump's executive orders to limit illegal entry to the US and expedite deportation, states and cities have become "sanctuaries," preaching states' rights philosophy reminiscent of the antebellum South.

A Gallup report in February 2019 indicated that millions in Latin

America were awaiting results of border wall funding—following the government shutdown and bipartisan conference to reach a compromise-- to decide when to come to US as illegals. In striking a bipartisan border deal in February 2019, Democrats argued that non-criminal "immigrants" should not be detained, defining illegal entry as non-criminal. Plain English was uprooted again.

What rights do illegals have? Not voting in general elections but their benefits expand daily. In March a House Republican-backed bill that said *"allowing illegal immigrants the right to vote devalues the franchise and diminished the voting power of United States citizens"* was almost unanimously (except for 6) nixed by House Democrats.

California Gov. **Gavin Newsome** asked the state legislature to expand health coverage for illegal immigrants, and New York City Mayor **Bill de Blasio** wants the city to spend another $100 million on public hospitals so illegals are treated at clinics rather than ERs. *"From this moment on in New York City,"* de Blasio said, *"everyone is guaranteed the right to health care—everyone."* Writes Matthew Continetti, editor of the *Washington Free Beacon*, in NR (2/11/19): *"Coastal and metropolitan Democrats increasingly represent individuals who cannot vote, do not pay income taxes, and are ineligible for military service and jury duty. This epiphany has led the progressive movement to begin to elide and subvert the distinction between citizens and noncitizens."*

The de Blasio $100 million initiative that guarantees illegals in New York City get basic medical care through doctors at city-run hospitals wasn't enough for progressive New York legislators unfazed by the state's declining revenue necessitating the governor's reduction in Medicare spending by $550 million. A bill introduced in February by state senator Gustavo Rivera (D-Bx) and Assemblyman Richard Gottfried (D-Man.)—both head health committees-- would require Albany to spend at least $532 million to allow undocumented residents to enroll in New York's "Essential" health-insurance plan. Illegals—more than 400,000 adults-- whose household incomes are under 200% of the federal poverty line would be eligible, and would pay *"small premium amounts,"* with taxpayers' footing most of the bill. Federal law prohibits illegals from receiving Medicaid. All children in New York, including illegals, currently can receive medical care under the Child Health Plus program.

The shift toward open borders of leftists has taken a decade. In 2007, presidential candidate **Hillary Clinton** said, "*I will not support driver's licenses for undocumented people and will press for comprehensive immigration reform that deals with all of the issues around illegal immigration, including border security and fixing our broken system.*" In 2015, Clinton changed her mind. "*The leftwing of the Democratic Party has embraced the concept of open borders all but explicitly. Its members establish sanctuary cities and states, issue driver's licenses to illegal immigrants, oppose the construction of border barriers, and call for the abolition of Immigration and Customs Enforcement (ICE)*", observes Continetti. Bernie Sanders' Medicare-for-all proposal (2016) includes illegals. Kirsten Gillibrand is fighting to abolish ICE and enact Medicare-for-all.

On 1/15/19, Manhattan District Court Judge Jesse M. Furman, an Obama appointee, blocked the Trump administration from asking a question in the 2020 census about citizenship. 18 Democratic AGs had filed suit to stop the inquiry. Howard Husock noted in *City Journal*: "*The foreign-born population exceeds 20 percent in more than 50 Democratic congressional districts; the comparable figure for Republican districts is 11. In the district of celebrity congresswoman Alexandria Ocasio-Cortez, 25 percent of residents are foreign-born non-citizens, according to the American Community Survey.*" Said Obama in his farewell address: "*Because for all our outward differences, we, in fact, all share the same proud title, the most important office in a democracy: citizen.*" Imagine in 2019 an Obama quote sounds like a Republican admonishment!

The case of jihadist Hoda Muthana, born in Alabama, daughter of a Yemeni diplomat father, radicalized on Twitter, fled to ISIS in Syria and called for killing Americans on social media, brought the notion of citizenship to the forefront. ISIS is now mordant. Muthana, just 24, had married her 3rd ISIS militant after the first 2 husbands were killed, had a son by the 2nd, and after being captured by Kurd forces, is now fed up living in a Syrian refugee camp. Secretary of State Mike Pompeo said she may not return to the US because she is not a US citizen. Nevertheless, it is her father's diplomatic status at the time of her birth that may determine whether or not she is a citizen in a lawsuit filed by Muthana. Andrew McCarthy says that a "*person who is an American citizen by birth may not have that citizenship revoked without her consent. In its 1973 Afroyim v. Rusk decision, the Supreme Court reasoned that the Constitution does not grant Congress the power to strip an American of citizenship because, in our system, the people are sovereign—the government serves us, it is not the source of our citizenship."* On February 24th, Secretary Pompeo reiterated on "Fox News Sunday," *"She's a non-citizen terrorist,"* and confirmed *"we have a strong legal basis"* for saying so.

We no longer hear Democrats say that citizenship carries responsibilities as well as privileges. On Fox News' "Watters World," the amusing host in one show interviewed college students about their knowledge of civics. Few had any. That sad fact was borne out by a recent survey conducted by the Woodrow Wilson National Fellowship Foundation of 41,000 Americans in all 50 states and Washington DC. The questions asked were mostly grade-school level and most avoided asking for easily forgotten dates (an exception: when was the Constitution written?). You had to name the president in World War I and World War II, the enemy in World War II, identify a few founding figures, and know something about the Constitution. Only in landlocked Vermont could a majority pass the history questions on a US citizenship exam (the pass rate was 53%). Louisiana residents bombed at 27% passing. New York came in 32nd (40% pass rate). Overall, 40% passed, but only 27% of those under 45. The sad conclusion by the foundation president Arthur Levine: *"Unfortunately, the Woodrow Wilson Foundation has validated what studies have shown for a century: Americans don't possess the history knowledge they need to be informed and engaged citizens."*

Democratic lawmakers who are also immigrants seem befuddled by the meaning of citizenship. They do not see themselves joining Americans but redefining America as an open-border country that must admit all who wish to come and, at the same time, live up to their notion of the American dream regardless of how violent or impoverished their country of origin. Rep. Ilhan Omar complained to CNN's Christiane Amanpour that immigrants like her *"went through years of vetting and went through the process of becoming citizens. I mean we have been fingerprinted, tested, more than any American has ever been who's born in this country."* Observed *City Journal's* Seth Barron (adapted for the *NYP*, 3/9/19), *"Like many on the left, Omar believes America's purpose is to admit immigrants and make them feel welcome."* Barron gives another example: Omar telling MSNBC's Rachel Maddow of illegals crossing the southern border *"to create an opportunity and provide for this nation, are acting more in the American tradition"* than those averse to open borders. So, the illegals are doing America a favor by coming here. Gives new meaning to chutzpah.

With the battle over a southern wall to reduce illegal crossings, few should have been surprised at the surge of migrants, more than 76,000--90% were Guatemalans--who illegally crossed the southern border in February 2019 seeking asylum, the highest number in 12 years. It's more than double the 36,751 held in February 2018. They trek north—many come by bus rather than foot or caravan-- mostly in families, told by smugglers that the "open sesame" shibboleth is "asylum," since, by law, families can't be detained for more than 20 days, and, by court rulings, deportations require lengthy procedures. Once asylum seekers are in the country and submit an application, only those considered dangerous are detained. According to Homeland Secretary Kirstjen Nielsen, 80% of migrants who claim asylum to a border agent gain entry to the US. When released from temporary housing with an immigration court date, half never file an asylum claim but disappear into the interior (Betsey McCaughey, *NYP*, 3/15/19).

"It is no coincidence that these two groups—unaccompanied minors and family units – are crossing the border at an alarming rate," Senator Lindsey Graham said on March 6th at a Senate Judiciary Committee hearing on border security. *"Our immigration laws require that both unaccompanied children and family units be released into the interior of the United States after apprehension."* Graham pointed out 2 loopholes in immigration law: (1) the Flores settlement agreement, which requires children or families *"to be released after 20 days in custody"*; and (2) the Trafficking Victims Protection Reauthorization Act, that requires unaccompanied alien children from noncontiguous countries to be released to Health and Human Services care facilities instead of being returned sent back to their countries of origin —which means kids from Canada and Mexico go home, but not kids from Central America. Senator Graham wants these loopholes fixed to permit longer detention of families and the return of kids from Central America. Customs and Border Protection (CBP) Commissioner Kevin McAleenan said 63% of illegal crossings would be addressed by fixing those loopholes to provide 6-8- week detentions while asylum applications are reviewed.

From October 1, 2018 to March 3, 2019, 268,044 migrants have been apprehended. Over the last 5 months, Graham said, there's been an almost 55% increase in the number of unaccompanied minors caught at the border, and an almost 340% increase in the number of families apprehended as compared to last year. *"These laws incentivize smugglers to exploit migrants,"*

Graham stated. The smugglers, who *"know our legal system,"* made $2.5 billion in 2018. *"Word of mouth and social media quickly gets back to those in the Northern Triangle countries* [Guatemala, Honduras, El Salvador], *that if you bring a child, you'll be successful,"* pointed out Brian Hastings, CBP chief of law enforcement operations. Hastings reported that since April 2018 there were about 2,400 cases in which migrants either falsely claimed to be related or lied about being under 18.

At a House Homeland Security hearing on March 6th, Nielsen detailed the *"humanitarian catastrophe"* -- the price paid by children along the arduous route north: rape is so common that US agents perform pregnancy tests of every girl 10 and older. *"The flow of families and children has become a flood. Over the past five years, we have seen a 620 percent increase in families, or those posing as families, apprehended at the border,"* she said. CBP forecast that the problem will get worse in the spring, when it's warmer.

Democrats, who talk of border security but authorize no effective measures, chastised Nielsen for Homeland separating kids from parents and keeping children in "cages." *"Yes or no, are we still putting children in cages?"* asked Committee Chairman Bennie Thompson (D-Miss.). *"To my knowledge, CBP never purposely put a child in a cage,"* Nielsen replied. Thompson persisted and Nielsen explained, *"Sir, they're not cages. They are areas of the border facility that are carved out for the safety and protection of those who remain there while they're being processed."* Rep. Bonnie Coleman (D-NJ) said a chain-link fence enclosure sounds like a dog cage. Nielsen insisted it's a detention space. Is a schoolyard where children play (some having an enclosure within the larger yard enclosure for jungle gyms) or baseball stadium a cage?

There's no crisis at the border, proclaim House Democrats who voted to revoke Trump's emergency declaration. They cited previously plummeting border arrests as evidence. However, illegal border crossings are now approaching levels not seen since the George W. Bush administration: in 2008, more than 700,000 were detained at the border, and nearly 600,000 in 2009. Only about 60 – 75% of released migrants seeking asylum attend their immigration hearings, according to DOJ data.

9 GIMME YOUR COUNTRY

"This is an invasion"—Rush Limbaugh on "Fox News Sunday," 2/17/19

Congress wants to revamp America. AOC introduces a fantasy list to end the energy sector within 10 years, retrofit all buildings with solar panels, supplant air travel with bullet-speed trains, provide a basic income for those unwilling to work, and offer free health care and education to all. This coercive socialist program would turn the premier capitalist country into another failed socialist/Marxist disaster. AOC admits government would be coercive. The Green dream is backed by several 2020 Democratic contenders: Senators Elizabeth Warren, Kamala Harris, Bernie Sanders, Cory Booker, and Kirsten Gillibrand.

A CNN poll following Trump's State of the Union address calling for unity and a border wall showed 59% of viewers had a "very positive" reaction to Feb. 5th speech, 17% had a "somewhat positive" reaction and 23% viewed it negatively. A CBS News survey found that 76% gave Trump a thumbs up. 72% approved of his ideas for immigration. In his speech, Trump declared, *"America will never be a socialist country."* Trump said no issue better *"illustrates the divide between America's working class and America's political class than illegal immigration."* Politicians and political donors have walls and guards while *"working-class Americans are left to pay the price of illegal immigration."* The left-of-the-aisle legislators dressed in suffragette white largely sat on their hands until Trump said women *"have filled 58 percent of the newly created jobs last year."* Surprised by the standing ovation, Trump said, *"You weren't supposed to do that!"* He noted that *"we also have more women serving in Congress than at any time."* Pelosi beckoned the remaining sitting minions to their feet to applaud their own success-- a record 127 women in the 116th Congress.

Following the State of the Union address, which the *Wall Street Journal* called a turning point for the president, Trump's approval soared while that of New York's Democratic politicians nose-dived. Trump's approval rating reached 52% (disapproval 47%), the highest since shortly after his January 20, 2017 inauguration (55%), according to a Rasmussen Daily Presidential Tracking Poll released on February 11th, attributable to the strong economy and his speech. A Gallup Poll found 59% are optimistic about their finances, the highest in 16 years. A Sienna College poll of 778 registered voters (February 4-7) showed that New York Governor Cuomo's favorability rating dipped from 51% in January to 43% in February, presidential aspirant Senator Kirsten Gillibrand dropped 4 points to 44%, while her negative rating rose from 31% to 34%, and Senate Minority Leader Chuck Schumer dropped from 53% to 47%, his worst showing in a Sienna poll. These favorable numbers for the president plummeted with the government shutdown. A USA Today/Suffolk University of voters between March 13-17 found that 50% agreed with Trump that the Mueller probe was a "witch hunt," 62% thought the House should not impeach Trump, yet 52% of these 1,000 registered voters had "little or no trust" in Trump's denial of collusion. By late March, CNN reported that 71% of the American public thought the economy was good.

To take over a different kind of America, Democratic presidential hopefuls need to deny the achievements and successes in Trump's revitalized America. They need to ignore job and wage growth and talk about the left-behinds as failed Georgian Democratic gubernatorial candidate Stacey Abrams did in the Democratic response to the State of the Union address. These are the facts that need to be disputed or downplayed, especially in the Midwest which gave Trump his margin of victory.

Job growth: employers created 304,000 jobs in January 2019. Wages rose 3.2% over the last 12 months (Betsey McCaughey, NYP, 2/6/19) In Jan. 2017, just before Trump took office, the CBO predicted only 94,000 jobs per month would be created in 2018. The actual gains were more than double that. *"What explains that change? Trump's tax cuts and broad-scale de-regulation,"* said New York's former Lt. Gov. McCaughey. Unpleasant facts remain: ¾ of non-disabled, working age food-stamp recipients without children to care for still don't work, even part-time. Dems keep talking about income-inequality and the people left behind despite job growth among blacks, Hispanics, and women.

Walls v. Open Borders

The open-borders crowd sees entry into the US of illegal Hispanics as a surge in potential Democratic voters needing government assistance. In calling the border crisis "an invasion," radio host Rush Limbaugh spoke of "*millions of people breaking the law*" and the Democratic Party wanting it because "*we have a political party that needs an underclass*" ("Fox News Sunday," 2/17/19). On February 9th, former judge and prosecutor Jeanine Pirro said on her Fox News show that open-border Democrats know they've lost Americans in their quest for power, so they're seeking illegals. It's all about power.

President Trump signed both the bipartisan border security bill that extends government funding through September and gives the president a pittance for border barriers, and a declaration of emergency at the border, on Friday, February 15th. The bill provides close to $1.4 billion for 55 miles of additional border fencing and reportedly $21 billion in military construction funds that could potentially be used for a border wall although that money must be used in support of the US armed forces. Other monies that acting Chief of Staff Mick Mulvaney said are available include $3.6 billion from military construction funds, $2.5 billion from Defense Department anti-drug activities, and $600 million from the Treasury Departments asset-forfeiture fund. Trump is seeking $8 billion in funds to cover several hundred miles of border.

The possible transfers of money from Pentagon accounts is complicated, explains Charles Savage, et. al. in the *Times* (2/20/19). Indeed, it is. First, Trump intends to spend $2.5 billion in DOD funds unrelated to his emergency proclamation. Only the 4th pot of money, Savage explains, involves the emergency-powers statute. The 1st pot is $1.4 billion that Congress approved for new border barriers in the spending bill agreed upon during the shutdown. The 2nd is $600 million from a Treasury Department asset forfeiture fund. The 3rd pot to fund the wall is $2.5 billion from a military counterdrug account authorized by Congress to support other agencies' efforts by constructing fencing and lighting to block international drug smuggling, which, the *Times* believes, does not permit land acquisition. Furthermore, since the military doesn't have that much money available, the account would be used as a "way station" for funds taken from other military programs. Although the Anti-Deficiency Act makes it a crime to spend in excess of congressional appropriation, the Trump administration claims it can move money into the Pentagon's counterdrug account under "general transfer authority" that Congress has given the defense secretary, but which prohibits transfer "*where the item for which funds are requested has been denied by the Congress.*"

The legal challenge by a coalition of 16 Democratic-controlled states, joined by the American Civil Liberties Union, might block such maneuvers. California Governor Gavin Newsom and California's AG are leading the pack (NY, NJ, Conn., Del., Md., Me., Va., Colo., Ill., Mich., Nev., Mn., NM, Ore., and HA) in a lawsuit filed on February 18th —where else? — in San Francisco federal court, the ultra-left 9th Circuit.

The *Times* notes that if the Courts rule that "*Congress has given the executive branch the authority to redirect funds, the appropriations committees cannot veto any particular exercise of that power.*" In an editorial, however, the *Times* usurps the court's role and presumptively declares the declaration of emergency unconstitutional (congressional Republicans are "*forced to choose between supporting and defending the Constitution*") and the emergency "bogus"— "*there is no border emergency*"—as well as, again using Speaker Nancy Pelosi's words, a "*power grab.*"

Democrats lined up behind Speaker Nancy Pelosi. On February 26th, the House voted to block the emergency declaration, 245-182, with 13 Republicans joining the Democrats.

The *Times* as usual mischaracterized similar actions of then-President Barack Obama: "*Mr. Obama did extend emergency declarations for several uncontroversial foreign policy matters and use executive orders (lawfully) to achieve policy goals.*" Not so lawful was his executive order to protect the "Dreamers" after Congress didn't pass immigration reform, even acknowledging he had no right to do so-- DACA remains in litigation--nor his diktats on education and the environment, many litigated, and some overturned by the Trump administration.

.	The president said he'd veto the resolution. 12 Senate Republicans gave Democrats the majority, 59-41, on March 14th to nullify Trump's emergency declaration, as a curb on executive power— *"This check on the executive is a crucial source of our freedom,"* said Lamar Alexander (TN) in a statement. The only Republican to defy Trump up for reelection next year is Susan Collins (ME). The other naysayers were Rand Paul (KY), Lisa Murkowski (Alaska), Mike Lee and Mitt Romney (UT), Jerry Moran (KN), Pat Toomey (PA), Rob Portman (OH), Roger Wicker (Miss.), Marco Rubio (FL), and Roy Blunt (MO). Congress can override the veto with a 2/3 majority. The House failed to override Trump's veto on March 26th.

On March 11th, the president's $4.7 trillion budget was released (deadline is October 1st): it slashes domestic spending by 5%, calls for cuts to Medicare, Medicaid and Social Security over the next decade, boosts defense spending, and asks for $8.6 billion to fund the wall that Democratic leaders continue to deprecate as an *"ineffective border wall."* Trump's proposal is based on a 2017 CBP plan to replace or build 722 miles of barriers that would cost $18 billion. Only 111 miles have been completed or are being built.

Those arguing the border crisis is not an emergency say that illegal crossings are down. In 2000, 1.6 million were arrested at the border; in 2018, 400,000 were arrested. But now the number is going back up to 60,000/month. In February 2019, more than 76,000 migrants seeking asylum, mostly from Guatemala, the majority parents with kids, crossed the border illegally, the highest number in 12 years, more than double the number in February 2018. It is true, as Republican strategist Karl Rove acknowledges ("Fox News Sunday, March 17, 2019), that families want to surrender to border agents and claim asylum. A wall would not stop them, but would stop the single men who sneak through.

In his State of the Union address, President Trump said that there were 206,000 criminal assault arrests in 2018 of illegal aliens. Tucker Carlson of Fox News (2/11/19) reported that in 2018 ICE arrested more than 120,000 for an additional crime besides illegal entry to the US, making the US a sanctuary country. 88% of illegal immigrants that ICE holds committed a crime other than illegal entry. An illegal alien can claim asylum by setting one foot on US soil. *"The nation doesn't control its own border; the fact that past presidents chose not to recognize that fact is hardly Trump's fault,"* reasoned a *New York Post* editorial (2/16/19), in arguing that because we're not at peak illegal immigration doesn't mean there's no emergency. Well, thanks to Congressional inertia, we're heading back to the peak.

The argument that the declaration of emergency is unconstitutional-- Senator Marco Rubio (R-FL) called the move *"violating the Constitution"* --rests on Article I of the Constitution that empowers Congress to appropriate monies. However, Congress passed the **1976 National Emergencies Act** that defines an emergency as *"a general declaration of emergency made by the president"*—circular reasoning that Yale law professor and NYU scholar Peter H. Schuck in a *New York Times* op-ed piece compares to Humpty Dumpty's exegesis to Alice: *"it means just what I choose it to mean—neither more nor less."* Schuck laments Congress's *"delegation to presidents of vast, essentially unconstrained power to declare national emergencies"* and the fact that Trump *"may actually possess the legal authority to require agencies to waste billions of dollars simply to fulfill a foolish campaign promise he thinks won him the election"* (2/18/19). The Act has led to 58 declarations of emergency, most of which were for foreign adventures, going back to Jimmy Carter.

White House senior policy advisor Stephen Miller, in an interview with Chris Wallace, spoke of the 4,000 troops currently amassed at the border, and explained that when the president said on national TV he didn't have to do "this," he meant that as a matter of national security the US can't have uncontrolled borders and that he could get the money without the declaration. *"I could do the wall over a longer period of time,"* Trump said. *"I didn't need to do this, but I'd rather do it much faster."*

Most illegal drugs come through points of entry, argue those opposed to the emergency declaration. However, as Kate Pavlich from Town Hall.com observed, there's nobody to monitor drugs coming through elsewhere. Does smuggling not occur if there's no one there to see it?

Rather than being what Pelosi calls an end-run around Congress, the emergency declaration is a legislative loophole large enough for a Sherman Tank. Democrats have long supported physical barriers at the border. Before the government partial shutdown, Trump tweeted out a short video presenting Democrats as hypocrites, with 3 undated clips of its leaders on border security. Senator **Chuck Schumer** (D-NY), now Minority Leader, says: *"illegal immigration is wrong, plain and simple;"* **Hillary Clinton** says, *"I voted* *numerous times when I was senator to spend money to build a barrier to try to prevent illegal immigrants from coming in;"* and then-Senator **Barack Obama** says, *"We simply cannot allow people to pour into the United States, undetected, undocumented, unchecked."* Conservative Rush Limbaugh, who objected to Obama's 2012 executive action on the Dreamers because Obama was *"furthering this existing problem,"* supports the declaration because Trump *"is doing what he has to do. The spending bill is outrageous."* However, if the process is legal it's not because the ends justify the means.

Dems claim the cost is too expensive. It's far cheaper, Betsey McCaughey argues, than the more than $3 billion Homeland spends a year caring for illegals at the border, plus the cost of Health and Human Services caring for unaccompanied teens in shelters, plus the costs of schooling and health care of migrants released into the interior (*NYS*, 3/15/19).

Sheltering migrants has become nigh impossible. In late March, Border Patrol officials in Texas acknowledged that so many had crossed the border, that it started releasing them. The DOJ reports that 39% skipped their initial court date in 2016. By late March, the El Paso, Texas border was at the *"breaking point,"* said CBP Commissioner Kevin McAleenan with a new group of Central American migrants heading to the border. McAleenan said that *"apprehensions are on pace to surpass 100,000 this month,"* with many trying to cross the border having serious injuries and illnesses. 4,000 migrants were apprehended in one day recently. Migrants were being sheltered under a bridge. President Trump on March 28th threatened to shut the border if Mexico, Honduras, Guatemala, and El Salvador continued to do nothing *"to help stop the flow of illegal immigrants"* to the US. Homeland's Kirstjen Nielsen disclosed a March 27th agreement with the 3 Central American countries to prevent migrant caravans from forming and to help combat gangs and human trafficking. She asked Congress for authority to deport undocumented unaccompanied minors from Central America who are overwhelming the system.

Trump's measures to curtail these costs have been stymied by the courts, particularly the infamous 9th Circuit. Trump's regulation that asylum-seekers proceed only through ports of entry was rejected by a district court judge in November. In March 2019 the court ruled that migrants who fail to convince border agents of the dangers back home have a "right" to a US court hearing.

That ruling won't withstand appeal, McCaughey writes, in view of a different circuit ruling in 2016 that entry to the US is a privilege and a border agent's decision is final—a decision the Supreme Court left standing. The longevity of Trump's "Remain-in-Mexico" program remains to be seen. A win for Trump: the USSC in a 5:4 decision on March 19th ruled that the feds could pick up convicted illegal aliens awaiting deportation and incarcerate them at any time after they got out of prison.

Then there's consistency in idiocy. If the wall is immoral today, then existing barriers are immoral. Yes, agrees celebrity loser **Robert O'Rourke**, speaking with MSNBC's Chris Hayes: *"Yes, absolutely. I'd take the wall down"*. Both Hillary and Obama as senators voted for 700 miles of fencing in 2006. Scalia Law School professor, FH Buckley writes in the *New York Post* of 2 walls at the San Diego border, one 10-foot high, the other 15 feet, which cut illegal border crossings from Tijuana by 95%. *"Tijuana has the world's highest rate of homicide. And Beto wants to take the wall down,"* notes Buckley.

O'Rourke, who declared his candidacy for 2020 in March, wants to tear down all our border barriers and Senator **Kirsten Gillibrand** (D-NY) agrees. *Reuter* reported that O'Rourke was once part of a hacker group and for a time in his teens had written as "Psychedelic Warlord." The reporter of that story sat on it until after the 2018 election against Senator Ted Cruz. There's no business, like show business. Senator **Cory Booker** (D-NJ) is proof: he's concentrating on the more important issue of fighting meat and dairy *"corporate interests"*: *"The tragic reality is this planet simply can't sustain billions of people consuming industrially produced animal agriculture."* Personally, I think O'Rourke, Gillibrand, Booker, and Warren are GOP plants to help Trump. Now there's a conspiracy worth investigating.

10 GIMME COLLUSION

"I'm not for impeachment"—Speaker Nancy Pelosi tells *The Washington Post* on
March 11, 2019.

Dump Trump Lives On

To preserve an unraveling progressive state, far-left candidates need to
defeat Donald Trump in 2020. Their sights, however, are still on removing
the president as illegitimate or treasonous or corrupt or on undoing his
effectiveness. As William Barr, the newly confirmed AG, took over the
Mueller probe that was winding up, as the bipartisan Senate Intelligence
Committee acknowledged it found no evidence of collusion between the
Trump campaign and Russian officials, as corrupt former FBI officials were
promoting their books, attempting to reclaim their sullied reputations, we
learned almost daily new details of the workings of the "deep state."

House Intelligence Committee Chairman **Adam Schiff** (D-CA) asserted
mid-February that there's evidence of collusion, albeit not direct evidence.
By the end of the month, Schiff vowed on ABC's "This Week": "*We will
obviously subpoena the report. We will bring Bob Mueller in to testify before Congress.
We will take it to court if necessary.*" Barr was said to want to avoid Comey's
error in exonerating Hillary Clinton while publicly criticizing her handling of
classified material. The Mueller report would likely include material that
needed to be redacted before it was made public: raw data on people who
have not been indicted, such as Donald Trump, Jr, grand jury testimony, and
classified material. Schiff wanted it all—how else to go after the president if

Mueller didn't deliver a finding of collusion or obstruction of justice. On Sunday, March 3rd, Schiff clarified on CBS's "Face the Nation" that by collusion he means old news-- Don Jr. responding to emails from a British publicist to get dirt from a Russian lawyer on Hillary—now spun by Schiff as *"direct evidence in the emails from the Russians through their intermediary offering dirt on Hillary Clinton as part of what is described in writing as the Russian government effort to help elect Donald Trump."* Schiff was also looking into whether *"the Russians have been laundering money through the Trump Organization."* Schiff was calling for a treasure hunt for Trump's taxes and financial deals. On March 14th, the House passed a resolution (420-0, 4 Republicans voting present) to make Mueller's report public (except for classified material) and for it to be sent to Congress.

DOJ guidelines bar indicting a sitting president. Democrats admit wanting to build a case to impeach Trump. The confused Chair of the House Judiciary Committee **Jerrold Nadler** (D-Man./B'klyn) didn't need Mueller's report to speak on Sunday, March 3rd, on ABC's "This Week," of having a case against Trump for *"obstruction of justice, corruption and abuse of power."* However, as he told AM radio host, John Catsimatidis, he wants to review the Mueller finding before deciding on whether to impeach Trump! Go figure. By mid-March, Nadler was agreeing with House Speaker Nancy Pelosi on the conditions for impeachment: *"it has got to be bipartisan, the evidence has to be overwhelming."*

Regardless of Mueller's conclusions, House investigative committees made it clear that they would continue the search for an impeachable offense. Hence, Nadler requested documents from 81 individuals and entities including Don Jr. and son Eric, CFO of the Trump Organization, Allen Weisselberg, Jared Kushner, former AG Jeff Sessions, and former White House counsel Doug McGahn. The House Judiciary Committee is looking for offers of pardons or tampering with witnesses as abuses of power. House committees also want records of Trump's conversations with Putin. That's executive privilege. This fishing trip will continue through the 2020 presidential election and thereafter. That's why there are 6 Democratic-controlled House committees in search of an impeachable offense. Oversight, my foot. More like partisan wanton soup.

The McCabe & Rosenstein Show

On a media tour, former deputy director of the FBI, **Andrew McCabe**, fired by AG Jeff Sessions in March 2018 for lying three times under oath to federal investigators, confirmed that after Sessions fired FBI Director **James Comey** in May 2017 on Deputy AG **Rod Rosenstein**'s recommendation, he met with DOJ officials including Rosenstein in order to recruit Cabinet members and the VP to oust Trump as "unfit" under the 25th Amendment, an issue he claimed Rosenstein raised.   In an interview with CBS's "60 Minutes," McCabe said he was so troubled by his conversations with Trump after Comey's firing that he began an investigation into whether that constituted obstruction of justice and opened a counterintelligence probe into possible links between the president and Russian agents.   Then serving as acting FBI director, McCabe wanted to ensure a Russia probe would not be quashed.   He thought Donald Trump might have won "*with the aid of Russia*" and might be a "*Russian asset*." He pointed to Trump's dismissal of US intelligence reports that North Korean missiles were aimed at the US, believing Putin's denial instead.

Trump did not threaten to disband the probe, nor did he.   But McCabe was troubled by Trump calling the probe into his campaign a "witch-hunt" and a "hoax."   Much of it, of course, is—not Russian interference in the election, but the phony dossier that was used to obtain FISA warrants and smear Trump.

On NBC's "Today" show on February 19th, McCabe said he informed Republican congressional leaders and the "Gang of Eight" (Senate Majority Leader Mitch McConnell, House Speaker Paul Ryan, Senate Intelligence Committee Chair Richard Burr, House Intel Chair Devin Nunes, Senate Minority Leader Chuck Schumer, Senate Intel Democrat Mark Warner, House Intel Democrat Adam Schiff, and Rep. Nancy Pelosi) of the counterintelligence probe opened after Trump fired Comey. "*No one objected*," McCabe said.

The mind-boggling sequence is this: Colluding with FBI and other DOJ officials, Rosenstein signs the last FISA warrant to spy on the Trump campaign based on the Steele dossier compiled by an anti-Trump former British spy and paid for by the Clinton campaign; recommends firing Comey for his handling of the Clinton email probe and then uses the firing as the basis of appointing special counsel Robert Mueller; and holds talks with McCabe twice about wearing a wire, and about using the 25th Amendment to oust a duly elected president.

The "60 Minutes" interview made it clear that *"First of all, Trump was obviously perfectly capable of discharging his duties; he just discharged them in a way alarming to McCabe and Rosenstein,"* observed Rich Lowry. Rosenstein oversaw the special counsel *"to investigate the possible crime to which he was a party"*— that actually was not a crime since the FBI continued the Russia investigation now made *"more serious by making the president an explicit target"* (*NYP*, 2/20/19). *Bloomberg's* Eli Lake calls upon Rosenstein to explain recommending firing Comey and then discussing *"the crisis created by Comey's firing."*

The DOJ statement denying McCabe's account echoed Rosenstein's denial in September 2018 when the *New York Times* published it: *"The Deputy Attorney General never authorized any recording that Mr. McCabe references. As the Deputy Attorney General has previously stated, based on his personal dealings with the President, there is no basis to invoke the 25th Amendment, nor was the DAG in a position to consider invoking the 25th Amendment."* Rosenstein, reportedly set to leave the DOJ in March, stayed on to assist AG Barr.

Process Crimes & Financial Crimes

Following the arrest of Trump confidante **Roger Stone**, Julie Pace of the *Associated Press* said (on "Fox News Sunday," 1/27/19) that she found no real connection to Trump or conspiracy with Russia. Stone allegedly was trying to coverup his communications to find out about the next WikiLeaks dump on Hillary. The Mueller probe has pinned "process crimes" on Stone-- allegedly lying to Congress and witness tampering-- and financial crimes-- tax evasion and bank fraud, related to his earnings as a consultant to a pro-Russia Ukrainian party--on **Paul Manafort**. AOC cried foul when Manafort was sentenced to less than 4 years in prison. In addition to the prison time from which his 9 months behind bars will be deducted, Judge TS Ellis III in Virginia ordered $25 million in restitution and $50,000 fine. In a separate sentencing on March 13th on charges of illegal foreign lobbying, obstruction of justice and money laundering, DC Judge Amy Berman Jackson gave Manafort 73 months, with 30 months overlapping his 47-month sentence in Virginia. In total, he'll spend 81 more months in prison.

The hatred by the Left of everything Trump is so great that Manhattan prosecutors got a grand jury on March 13th to indict Trump's former campaign manager on state residential mortgage fraud, conspiracy, falsifying business records, and other state charges that can't be pardoned by President Trump. The trick is for Manhattan DA Cyrus Vance Jr. to evade double-jeopardy laws, according to *Bloomberg News*. Legal eagle Jonathan Turley at *The Hill* calls the effort to charge Manafort with state crimes based on the same illegal activities "*blind rage*," not justice.

The collusion unveiled thus far, as Trump has often noted, has been among anti-Trump law enforcement officials. Rush Limbaugh called the FBI and DOJ attempts to remove Trump a "*silent coup*"—unelected people decided that the American people's decision was "*invalid*." Like Trump, he calls the Mueller probe into the Trump campaign a "hoax" ("Fox News Sunday," 2/17/19) that has nabbed people engaged in "*process crimes*" that make it "*look like there was collusion*." These convictions, says the radio host, are part of the "deep state" attempt to get Trump's approval ratings down. Even Fox News panelist Charles Lane of the liberal *Washington Post* said "*it's way above their pay grade to discuss which cabinet member would invoke the 25th Amendment*." He wondered "*who is really watching*" the watchers.

The double standard is glaring. President Obama whispers to a Russian official that he'll be more flexible in his 2nd term and nobody cares. The $145 million contribution by Russians to the Clinton Foundation doesn't even raise media eyebrows, let alone merit an investigation.

In view of McCabe's attempted "*bureaucratic coup*," Senate Judiciary Committee Chairman **Lindsey Graham** (R-SC) wants McCabe to testify about DOJ "*bias against Trump*." AG Bill Barr will likely be called on to investigate these politicized officials in the FBI and DOJ, including the FBI agents who investigated both the Trump campaign and Hillary email case, and the abuses by officials obtaining surveillance warrants from the secret FISA court. On March 17th, President Trump blasted new revelations that John McCain, who died last August, "*sent the Fake Dossier to the FBI and Media hoping to have it printed BEFORE the Election. He & the Dems, working together failed (as usual). Even the Fake News refused this garbage!*"

<u>The Cohen Circus</u>

The flurry of news reports on alleged Trump wrongdoing in February 2019 seemed geared to keep his feet to the fire as media focus shifted from collusion to obstruction of justice. On February 20, 2019, the *New York Times* headlined Trump's alleged request to acting AG Matt Whitaker to appoint Trump-ally Jeff Berman to head the Manhattan prosecution of former Trump lawyer Michael Cohen. Not giving up its sacred calling to find something with which to impeach President Trump, the *Times* devoted a front-page spread on February 20th to its contention that where there's smoke, there's fire. The headline was "*Inside Trump's Angry War On Inquiries Around Him.*" Imagine if Alfred Dreyfus's protestations of innocence in the notorious French anti-Semitic frameup more than a century ago had deterred Emile Zola from rebutting it with "*J'accuse.*" The *Times* cited lawyer Michael Cohen's testimony regarding hush money to 2 women in the 2016 campaign and the charge that Matt Whitaker was asked to put a Trump crony in charge of the case, which was denied by Whitaker and Trump.

TV networks ran clips of Whitaker's testimony before the House Judiciary Committee in which he emphatically denied ever being asked to intervene in the Mueller or any other probe. Talking heads gleefully opined that the House committee under Rep. Jerry Nadler (D-NY) would seek perjury charges. Speaking to a Navy Seal on February 15th, CBS News war correspondent Lara Logan blasted journalists for becoming "*political activists*" and "p*ropagandists*" who put out stories "*based on one official, former administration official.*" "*That's not journalism. That's horseshit,*" she declared, citing the critique of the *Times* by its former editor, Jill Abramson, for its negative coverage of Trump.

In the runup to deliverance of the Mueller report came the explosive public testimony of Trump's former personal attorney and fixer **Michael Cohen** before the House Oversight Committee on Wednesday, February 27, 2019, while the president was at a summit in Vietnam with North Korean dictator Kim Jong-un, timed to embarrass Trump. Cohen leavened his public testimony with name-calling of the president in an opening statement, much of which was leaked ahead of time to the media.

If you were a Trump-hater watching the spectacle you got some pleasure from the sleazy disbarred attorney convicted in August 2018 of tax evasion, campaign-finance violations, and lying to Congress smear his former boss. He was "*ashamed*" that he worked for Trump because "*he* is *a racist. He is a con man. He is a cheat.*" He claimed that he turned on Trump because of his failure to denounce the Charlottesville riot and his rejection of US intelligence assessments in his Helsinki meeting with Putin. None of this was a surprise to Trump supporters or haters. People who support Trump put aside his character flaws, just as they did for Bill Clinton.

Cohen faces 3 years in prison, he can't practice law in New York, he never got a White House job, and was left on his own to face the wrath of Mueller. Rep. Carolyn Maloney told "Good Day New York" (3/1/19) he had no reason to lie. He had every reason. A man scorned, which he denied under oath: "*I did not want to go to the White House*," he told Rep. Jim Jordan (R-Ohio). CNN's Dana Bash said she'd been told, "*he very much wanted a job in the White House.*" The *Wall Street Journal* in 2018 had reported that he had expected to be Trump's campaign chief and White House chief of staff. The very next day GOP Reps. Jim Jordan (OH) and Mark Meadows (NC) sent a letter to AG Barr requesting he charge Cohen with perjury. Among his false statements were his claim that he never wanted a White House job, that he "*never defrauded any bank*," and that he denied any foreign government ties. Cohen's damaged credibility got smashed to pieces when another seeming lie surfaced: Cohen's lawyer Lanny Davis said on March 6th that Cohen did consider seeking a pardon last year as part of a joint defense agreement Cohen had with the president after Cohen's office was raided in April 2018; the joint defense ended in July 2018. Discussion of a pardon was broached by Cohen's then-lawyer Stephen Ryan. This admission contradicts Cohen's testimony before the House Oversight Committee: "*I have never asked for, nor would I accept, a pardon from Mr. Trump.*"

Then there are the book and movie contracts that Cohen's been enticed with. "Stand by Your President" won't sell. Democrats don't talk about the millions leaking Comey has made as a born-again resistance fighter. Wrote Michael Goodwin: "*For his efforts, which included a book and coming out of the closet as an anti-Trump partisan, Comey has become a millionaire several times over*" (NYP, 2/24/19). McCabe, fired for lying under oath to IG investigators and reportedly still under investigation, has found redemption in a book tour. On release from prison, Cohen will undoubtedly market his obsequious mea culpas into guest spots on talk shows and perhaps even into a steady gig on

MSNBC. Since becoming a registered Democrat, a penitent Cohen has been genuflecting to the "resistance." Cohen will need the money, especially if he doesn't win his lawsuit against the Trump Organization for nearly 2 million in unpaid legal fees.

If you are a Trump-hater wanting immediate grounds for impeachment, you were disappointed. Cohen had no evidence of collusion, merely "suspicions." No mention of obstruction of justice. He denied the fraudulent Steele dossier's claim (in a report dated Oct. 20, 2016) in which an unidentified "*Kremlin insider*" told a friend Cohen had "*secret meetings with Kremlin officials in August 2016*," and denied ever being in Prague, refuting a key allegation in the dossier that alleged an "*extensive conspiracy*" between the Trump campaign and Russia, used to launch the FBI probe into the Trump campaign. Cohen also testified that he had no direct evidence that Trump knew Don Jr. was going to meet with a Russian asset at Trump Tower in June 2016. Cohen also denied ever receiving a direct order from Trump to lie to Congress about the timetable of Trump's discussions with Moscow about building a skyscraper. "*Mr. Trump did not directly tell me to lie to Congress*"—which would have constituted suborning perjury, an impeachable offense--testified Cohen, although he "*understood*" he was to lie.

As to the WikiLeaks dump, Cohen was present when Roger Stone related to Trump that Julian Assange had told him that WikiLeaks would release more hacked Democratic emails in July 2016 that would hurt Hillary's campaign. No crime there on Trump's part. Republicans insist the plan had been reported in a British newspaper a month earlier. As to the more salacious rumors, Cohen denied that there was a tape of Trump striking Melania, and said the president wouldn't have done so.

Herein lies the danger for Trump: as part of his Manhattan plea deal, Cohen had to plead that Trump directed a "*criminal scheme to violate campaign-finance laws*" in hiding the payoffs to porn star Stormy Daniels and former Playboy model Karen McDougal. McDougal was paid $150,000 through the *National Inquirer*, while Cohen paid Daniels $130,000. There is nothing illegal about such nondisclosure agreements, writes former prosecutor Andrew McCarthy (*NR*, 3/25/19), but their proximity to the election led prosecutors to see the McDougal payoff "*as an illegal corporate contribution*," and the Daniels payment "*exceeded Cohen's personal contribution limit*," and neither was disclosed to the FEC. Furthermore, Trump's reimbursements to Cohen left him with "*a pending debt to Cohen in 2017*," that was not on his financial-disclosure form, which the New York AG is looking at as possible accounting fraud by the Trump Organization. Since early February, the Southern District of New York has been conducting a probe of the Trump Inaugural Fund, in pursuit of charges of conspiracy, fraud, and money laundering (a Ukrainian had donated $50,000 although foreign contributions are illegal).

For those Trump-haters who, like a spider, can bide their time, some of the questions put to Cohen suggest that the Manhattan DA may find more fodder in Trump's business dealings and taxes. AOC asked about the accuracy of a 2016 *Washington Post* report that said $127 million in taxpayer funds were used to build his public golf course in the Bronx, while he gets to keep the profits. Cohen replied, "*It's identical to what he did at the Trump National Golf Club at Briarcliff Manor.*"

All in all, not a good day for Trump. It could have been much worse.

The Cohen hearings were "*the first step*" in House oversight of all Trump doings, declared Rep. Debbie Dingle (D-MI) on "Fox News Sunday" (3/3/19). The president isn't paranoid. They're really out to get him.

Speaker Pelosi confessed on Monday, March 11th to the *Washington Post*, "*I'm not for impeachment.*" She explained, "*Impeachment is so divisive to the country that unless there's something so compelling and overwhelming and bipartisan, I don't think we should go down that path, because it divides the country.*" She added, "*And he's just not worth it.*" What she didn't say was that a partisan hatchet job would not pass the Senate and would boomerang for her party in 2020. "High crimes and misdemeanors" do not include impulsive crude proclamations or flattery of dictators or conservative policies or denigration of illegal aliens—unless a majority in the House says it does. All hell broke loose when Mueller delivered his report to AG Barr.

The Finale—Or Is It?

On Friday, March 22nd, the Mueller report on Russian meddling in the 2016 election was submitted to AG Barr. DOJ officials said Mueller did not recommend any further indictments. Nearly 3 dozen individuals and 3 companies had been criminally charged. The 25 indicted Russians (for online disinformation and social media manipulation by the Internet Research Association—IRA-- and for hacking Democratic emails) will never stand trial. Not a single American of the 6 charged in the Trump campaign (Michael Flynn, Paul Manafort, Rick Gates, Roger Stone, George Papadopoulos, Michael Cohen) has been charged with criminally conspiring with the Russians. The FISA wiretap of Carter Page, undertaken for political not security reasons, yielded nothing of consequence. It is up to Barr, who has promised transparency, to decide what parts of the Mueller report get redacted—such as classified information-- and what is made public. Rep. Adam Schiff was quick to threaten Mueller with a subpoena if he does not get every word and comma. The more than $30 million extravaganza of nearly 2 years—19 lawyers, 40 intelligence and forensic experts, 500 witness, nearly 3,000 subpoenas-- made a liar of high-ranking Democrats and CNN and MSNBC talking heads who promised that the president's head and those of campaign aides would roll.

On Sunday, Barr sent a 4-page summary, written with the assistance of Rod Rosenstein, who appointed Mueller, of the more than 300-page report to the Senate and House Judiciary Committees. Mueller found no evidence of Trump campaign "collusion" with Russia: *"The Special Counsel did not find that any US person or Trump campaign official or associate conspired or knowingly coordinated"* with Russians *"despite multiple offers from Russian-affiliated individuals to assist the Trump campaign."* Mueller had informed Barr 3 weeks prior to the report's release that it would not reach a conclusion about whether Trump obstructed justice, the DOJ informed the *AP*. Barr said Mueller's findings were *"not sufficient to establish that the President committed an obstruction of justice offense."* Barr wrote: *"In cataloguing the president's actions, many of which took place in public view"*—firing Comey, disparaging the probe— *"the report identifies no actions that, in our judgment, constitute obstructive conduct, had a nexus to a pending or contemplated proceeding, and were done with corrupt intent."* So, while the Mueller report doesn't exonerate the president on obstruction charges, Barr and Rosenstein concluded there was no obstruction: *"I have concluded that the evidence developed during the Special Counsel's investigation is not sufficient to establish that the President committed an obstruction-of-justice offense".*

Dems were having none of it. Party leaders would not concede that an innocent president had been accused of treason. All wanted to see the full report and raw data and took aim at the previously sainted Barr as a partisan hack, as if he would misrepresent Mueller's findings while the special counsel remained silent. All found fault with Mueller passing the buck on obstruction to a political appointee—Barr.

Should obstruction even have been considered? Harvard Law Professor Alan Dershowitz said it was Mueller's job to decide the issue. If the president acts within authority, you don't look at intent, he explained on Martha MacCallum's "The Story" (Fox News, 3/25/19). You look at his actions and only look at intent if his actions are unlawful. Several commentators noted that you can't have obstruction of justice without an underlying crime. Conservative *NR* editor Rich Lowry noted that Trump fired Comey because the FBI director refused to state publicly *"what he told Trump privately—that the president himself wasn't under investigation"* (*NYP*, 3/26/19). Trump acted aggrieved, with snide remarks, *"basically told that he'd be investigated and smeared for years over Russian collusion that didn't happen, and if he objected and wanted to make it stop, they'd investigate him for that, too."*

House Judiciary Chairman **Jerrold Nadler** said his role differs from the Special Counsel that looks for crimes. Nadler demanded all raw data to look for *"abuse of power"* and *"obstruction of justice."* The Dems who have hidden findings on IRS abuse, Operation Fast and Furious, and Benghazi investigations suddenly wanted "transparency"—meaning raw material even on those not indicted. House Intel Chair **Adam Schiff**, privy to classified material, has peddled lie after lie about Trump "collusion." Representative Mike Conaway (R-TX) read a letter signed by the 9 GOP members on the committee calling on Schiff to resign because of his *"willingness to continue to promote a demonstrably false narrative."* Undeterred, Schiff cited questionable contacts by the Trump campaign (such as Don Jr.'s Trump Tower meeting with a Kremlin-connected lawyer in June 2016) and called Trump compromised and unethical. Another battle looms. However, the *"only campaign that took information from Russia,"* said former Rep. Trey Gaudy, *"is the campaign"* Adam Schiff supported.

Other Trump's defamers did not apologize. Rep. Eric Swalwell (D-CA) called the president a foreign agent on CNN (12/13/18): *"It's looking more and more that Donald Trump was a part of a criminal campaign, a criminal transition, and now resides over a criminal conspiracy."* Senator Richard Blumenthal (D-CN) said on MSNBC (3/21/19) days before submission of the Mueller report: *"There are indictments in this president's future.*" The president called the behavior of senior FBI agents "treasonous." The FBI made no effort to corroborate the Steele dossier even after the FISA application. Comey confided some salacious allegations to president-elect Trump but neglected to tell him that campaign aides were suspected of collusion with Russia. The bias and duplicity of senior FBI officials—Comey, McCabe, Strzok, Lisa Page—continue to boggle the mind.

Following release of Barr's summary, the mainstream media were on "*life support,*" as the president put it. TV news anchors and "analysts" were in shock. Pundit **John Brennan** was head of the CIA when he went on TV and called Trump guilty of "treason." Senator Rand Paul's bombshell allegation was that no one in the intelligence community was paying attention to the Steele dossier, so Brennan attached it to the intel report. The dossier became the heart of the FISA warrant. Rep. Peter King (R-NY) said Brennan "*is the evil force*" (Fox News, 3/18/19). Brennan now claims to have been given faulty information.

Dershowitz, who describes himself as "*a liberal Democrat,*" revealed that CNN "*wouldn't have me on the air*" because of his legal rather than partisan opinions. He believes the FISA court should call to task the people who lied.

Sometime in April the Mueller report, redacted where necessary, will be released. Meanwhile the DOJ's Inspector General Michael Horowitz's probe of FISA abuse and leaking of classified information by former FBI Director James Comey is expected to wrap up in late spring. Among several Republican leaders, Senate Judiciary Chair **Lindsey Graham** wants an investigation of what and who prompted the Trump campaign probe. An early victim was **George Papadopoulos**, then a minor Trump policy adviser, who regrets pleading guilty in October 2017 to lying about his interactions with British professor Joseph Mifsud, who claimed the Russians had dirt on Hillary. He spent 12 days in jail. He has written a book about attempts to ensnare him in collusion allegations, and says, "*There should be a new investigation into the prior Obama administration. I hold Obama responsible for this Russia probe.*" Foreign spies he met abroad were tape-recording him and baiting him with questions about Russia. How high in the Obama administration did the plot go to surveil the Trump campaign, slander the president-elect as a foreign agent, and effect a bureaucratic coup? Only more subpoenas to John

Brennan, Loretta Lynch, Sally Yates, Rod Rosenstein, and Barack Obama will tell.

ABOUT THE AUTHOR

RH Cheval is the author of children's stories, plays, mysteries, and political and historical commentaries, most recently *Political Apostates* and *Hate Crimes: Who's to Blame?*

www.ingramcontent.com/pod-product-compliance
Lightning Source LLC
Chambersburg PA
CBHW051352280526
45784CB00007B/2916